CHRISTOPHER CULPIN

THE RUSSIAN REVOLUTION

HODDER
EDUCATION
AN HACHETTE UK COMPANY

The author and publisher wish to thank Matthias Neumann for his advice as Academic Consultant and Joanne Philpott for her advice and support. All judgements, interpretations and errors remain the responsibility of the author.

The Schools History Project

Set up in 1972 to bring new life to history for students aged 13–16, the Schools History Project continues to play an innovatory role in secondary history education. From the start, SHP aimed to show how good history has an important contribution to make to the education of a young person. It does this by creating courses and materials which both respect the importance of up-to-date, well-researched history and provide enjoyable learning experiences for students.

Since 1978 the Project has been based at Trinity and All Saints University College Leeds. It continues to support, inspire and challenge teachers through the annual conference, regional courses and website: http://www.schoolshistoryproject. org.uk. The Project is also closely involved with government bodies and awarding bodies in the planning of courses for Key Stage 3, GCSE and A level.

For teacher support material for this title, visit www.schoolshistoryproject.org.uk.

Although every effort has been made to ensure that website addresses are correct at time of going to press, Hodder Education cannot be held responsible for the content of any website mentioned in this book. It is sometimes possible to find a relocated web page by typing in the address of the home page for a website in the URL window of your browser.

Hachette UK's policy is to use papers that are natural, renewable and recyclable products and made from wood grown in sustainable forests. The logging and manufacturing processes are expected to conform to the environmental regulations of the country of origin.

Orders: please contact Bookpoint Ltd, 130 Milton Park, Abingdon, Oxon OX14 4SB. Telephone: +44 (0)1235 827720. Fax: +44 (0)1235 400454. Lines are open 9.00a.m.–5.00p.m., Monday to Saturday, with a 24-hour message answering service. Visit our website at www.hoddereducation.co.uk.

© Christopher Culpin 2012
First published in 2012 by
Hodder Education,
an Hachette UK company
338 Euston Road
London NW1 3BH

Impression number   10 9 8 7 6 5 4 3 2 1
Year   2016 2015 2014 2013 2012

Typeset in 10pt Usherwood Book
Design by Lorraine Inglis Design
Artwork by Oxford Designers and Illustrators and Barking Dog
Printed and bound in Italy

A catalogue record for this title is available from the British Library
ISBN 978 1 4441 4456 7

Contents

The Russian Empire in 1900

Arkhangelsk

Finland

Kronstadt · St. Petersburg*

Novgorod

Pskov

Ekaterinburg

Moscow

Ural Mountains

Mogilev

Tambov

Samara

GERMANY

Poland

Kiev

Ukraine

Tsaritsyn**

AUSTRIA–HUNGARY

Odessa

Black Sea

Batumi

Caspian Sea

Tashker

Baltic Sea

------ Trans-Siberian Railway

* renamed Petrograd from 1914
  and Leningrad from 1924

** renamed Stalingrad from 1925

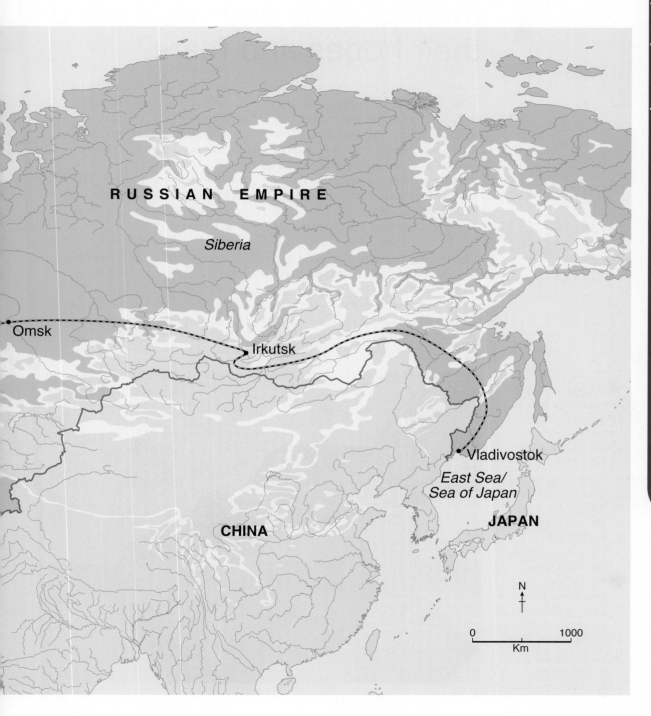

RUSSIAN EMPIRE

Siberia

Omsk

Irkutsk

Vladivostok

*East Sea/
Sea of Japan*

CHINA

JAPAN

N

0   1000
Km

1 Russia in 1900: Who were the Russians and what were their hopes and fears?

Today, Russia is the biggest country in the world. If you intend to visit Irkutsk, for example, the biggest city in far-eastern Russia, you face a five-hour flight eastwards from Moscow, passing through six time-zones. The Russian Empire of 1900, which is when this book starts, was even bigger – and there were no aeroplanes then!

There were, however, railways, and in 1900 Russia was finishing the greatest railway-building scheme in the world: the Trans-Siberian Railway. 90,000 workers toiled for 12 years to complete the 6000 km long track from Vladivostok in the far east to Moscow in the west.

The best way of getting a sense of the size of Russia is to use a globe. The map on the previous pages shows the places named in this book, and the Trans-Siberian Railway.

If you were a British visitor travelling, not the whole journey, but just the 2200 km westwards from Omsk to St Petersburg in 1900: what would the view from the windows of the train tell you about Russia in 1900?

■ As you read about this journey make a list of the groups of people you see, hear about and meet on this journey.

- What do you think are the hopes and fears of the men and women in each group?
- Does it seem likely that their hopes can be met, and their fears set aside, as Russia moves into the twentieth century?
- What obstacles might there be to achieving their hopes?

△ This photograph along with the other remarkable colour photographs in this chapter were taken by Sergei Prokudin-Gorsky between 1909 and 1915.

Setting out

It's a three-day journey, so there's plenty of time to watch Russia go past. At first it just seems empty, especially on the first day. There are enormous pine forests, through which the train chugs for what seems like hours. There are woods of tall silver birches, and long open stretches of grassy plain. For a couple of hours you pass through a range of mountains, with bare rocky peaks and steep forested slopes. These are the Urals, seen by some as the eastern boundary of Europe. But mainly the land is almost, but not quite, flat, rolling gently away into the distance.

Most of Russia's great rivers run north–south, so every so often the train rattles across huge bridges (as in the photograph on page 4). If they look a bit familiar it is because some were designed, and even made, in sections, in Britain.

The peasants

Where are the Russians? A country is its people, not just its geography. Gradually, increasingly as you travel west from the Urals, you see signs of human activity. It is June, and when the train goes past a field, you can see that the hay harvest is in full swing. Dozens of men, women and children are working in the fields, the men in long shirts, belted at the waist, the women in long dresses and colourful headscarves.

▽ Getting in the hay harvest. Men and women are working together. In Russia's climate the growing season is short, so everyone was needed to help with the harvest. You can see that all the work is being done by hand, with wooden tools and wooden wagons. All these items, and their clothes, would be made by the peasants themselves. They were almost self-sufficient, needing only a few manufactured items, such as the metal for the blades of their scythes.

Occasionally you pass close to a village (like the one in the photograph). These look even more antiquated. Is this 1900, or 1300?

▷ Study this picture – peasants like these, living in villages like this one, made up 82 per cent of the Russian people. Their lives changed relatively little during the period covered by this book. Notice the small wooden huts, lanes deep in baked mud, barefoot children and shabbily-dressed women.

You decide to get some lunch from the grumpy attendant at the end of your carriage. As you collect your smoked fish, bread and little glass of tea, you get talking with another passenger. He tells you that, indeed, these really are the Russian people – the peasants, 82 per cent of the population, living in hundreds of thousands of little villages all over the country. He points out that their apparent shabbiness is because they make nearly all of their own clothes, including shoes, from the things they grow and weave themselves. They also make all their own houses, furniture, plates, spoons, cups and ornaments, of wood. They eat only what they produce themselves, too. Any surplus, of grain, or cheese, or eggs, they take to market to exchange for the three things they need and cannot produce for themselves: salt, to preserve food, metal for tools, and vodka. Apart from these, the village is self-sufficient: they even treat their own illnesses themselves, with traditional herbal remedies prepared by the village-healer – the *znakharka*. They have lots of village traditions and rituals, some of them still believe in quite **pagan** superstitions.

pagan
The belief in good and evil spirits, outside Orthodox Christian Church teachings

The community of the *mir*, the village, is everything. Women use sickles to cut the winter wheat, or rye, while the men use scythes to cut the spring-sown crops. The women tie the grain into sheaves while the men start the ploughing. While the men sow seed for next year's crop, women carry the grain to the barns to be threshed.

These men, with their beards, boots and padded coats, are the village elders, meeting to take decisions together about village life. The only people from outside who affected their lives were the landowner and the local government official. Both took money from them, as debt repayments or taxes, and they hated both of them. It was a profound peasant belief that they ought to have more land, and landowners had more than enough. They had worked on the land for generations, so had earned the right to it and knew best how to farm it.

By far the most important things in the *mir* are the land, the crops and the animals. The peasants elect their own officials to organise the farming: when to plough, when to sow, when the harvest should start, and deal with any disputes. As you pass one village, your new friend points out just such a meeting: a group of elderly male peasants arguing round a table (see the photograph above).

'Are they happy?' you ask.

'Probably happy enough,' he replies, 'but that doesn't stop them grumbling most of the time.'

He explains that the population of Russia has been rising fast. It was only 48 million in 1800, now it is 125 million. Everyone in the *mir* believes that they have to look after each other, so the land is divided up and sub-divided, with the result that each family has less and less to live off. They are all hungry for more land, and look angrily at the big estates of the nobles. In fact, until 1861 the peasants themselves were owned by the nobles, as serfs or slaves. Now they own their own land, but have huge debts to pay for it.

This sounds more like 1300 than 1900, but you can see his sympathy for the peasants, even though he obviously isn't one himself, and tell him so.

'I love the Russian peasants, and they make me weep,' he confesses. 'I have travelled in Britain and studied your farming methods. Do you know that your British farmers produce four times as much from the same amount of land as these peasants we glimpse out of the window? And they won't change their ways.' He explains that they still divide up the land into strips, so that each person gets a share of good and bad soil. A full third of the land lies unused (fallow) every year, to restore its fertility.

A vague memory of lessons on English medieval peasants surfaces in your mind.

He goes on: 'They're not interested in better seed, new machines, new breeds of livestock, fertilisers. It is the older peasants who make the decisions, and they will always resist anything which is different from the way they have always done things. Back in 1892 the crops in many areas failed, there was a famine and lots of people starved to death.'

The nobility

Just then a quite extraordinary sight appears.

△ It is not surprising that this country house looks as if it belongs in England,
France or Italy. The Russian nobility consider themselves to be Europeans:
they travel a lot in western Europe, and speak French or English as much as
Russian. They are well-informed about European styles of architecture,
fashion, literature and ideas.

It is like an English stately home, here in the Russian countryside. Your
companion explains that it must be the country estate of a wealthy noble.
Although they make up only 1 per cent of the population, the top Russian
nobility own 25 per cent of the land. The family who own this one
probably have a palace in St Petersburg as well. These are the people who
run Russia: they attend Tsar Nicholas II at court, hold all the important jobs
in the government and the civil service. Their sons fill the top officer ranks
in the smartest regiments in the army.

'Remember that we have nothing like your parliament,' says your new
friend. 'The government of Russia is the Tsar, and the tiny group of
aristocrats he chooses to carry out his orders. Of course, not all the nobility
live like that, nor wield so much power. There's a much larger group of
nobles who are not so well off, and live in the countryside like gentleman
farmers. In fact some of them really know what they're doing. They've
taken advantage of the coming of railways to modernise their farms to
grow wheat and cotton and sell them for good prices.'

'You always bring it back to agriculture,' you comment.

'Well, although we are industrialising fast now, Russia is still way behind your country and Germany. And I must confess that agriculture is my business. I am an adviser on agriculture to a *zemstvo* just a bit further up the line.'

'What is a *zemstvo*?'

'They are elected local councils, a bit like your county and rural district councils.'

'So you do have democracy locally?'

'In a way. When Nicholas II's grandfather, Tsar Alexander II, introduced *zemstva* in 1864, he arranged the system of voting to favour the nobility. They fill 70 per cent of the seats in the provincial *zemstvo* and 40 per cent in the local *zemstvo*. At least it's more democratic than at the national level where there's no power-sharing at all. And we are getting things done. We are building schools and employing teachers. Our doctors are bringing modern medicine to the peasants. Then I do my best to persuade the peasants to adopt more modern agricultural ideas. It's an uphill struggle, though. The Tsar and his advisers are suspicious of people like me because they hate any change. In 1890 the Tsar's father, Alexander III, cut back the powers of the *zemstva*, giving his own provincial governors the power to overrule us."

He leans towards you and whispers: 'His son, our Tsar Nicholas II, is no better. He thinks he can stop the clock and rule Russia as if he was the medieval Tsar of Muscovy. But change will come: there are 100 million peasants in this country, and no one really understands what makes them tick. If they decide to move, they will be brutal and unstoppable. Or we can try to turn these medieval peasants into successful modern farmers, with a vested interest in peaceful progress, like I and my friends in the *zemstvo* are trying to do.'

'Why are you whispering?'

'What I've just said is dangerous talk. The Tsar's secret police, called the *Okhrana*, are everywhere. That man down the carriage is pretending to read his newspaper, but I'm sure he's trying to listen to what we're saying. Fortunately we're nearly at my station, so I'll get my things together and say goodbye!'

You shake hands and wave goodbye, and new passengers take their seats on the train.

The Church

Sitting opposite you now is a Russian Orthodox priest, a tall man, dressed in long black robes, with a big crucifix round his neck, a huge black beard and long hair tucked into his high black hat. You had noticed that by far the most prominent building in all the villages and small towns you've passed through was the church, often with a bell-tower topped with an onion-shaped dome.

△ A Russian Orthodox church towering over the rooftops of the town of Batumi. The Russian Orthodox Church is a Christian Church, neither Roman Catholic nor Protestant, adapted from the Greek Orthodox Church back in 988 AD. It was very powerful: from the **Patriarch** in St Petersburg to the local priest or monastery, the Church's presence was everywhere. It ran most schools, acted as a censor and was a dedicated supporter of the Tsar.

Patriarch
Head of the Russian
Orthodox Church

You comment on this to the priest, who glowers at you, but tells you confidently in broken English that Russians are very religious people.

'The Russian Orthodox Church owes nothing to anyone outside this Holy Land of Russia. Our Church is the Russian people at prayer. The singing in our churches is a high point of Russian culture and our icons a supreme achievement of Russian art. Every peasant, however poor, has an icon corner in their hut. Every peasant loves his village priest and willingly pays the dues necessary to him.'

You're not sure this can be true, but instead you ask him: 'What do you teach your people?'

'I teach them that it is their religious duty to obey those in authority as they obey God, because it is God who has chosen them. Most of all they must obey the Tsar, who was anointed to lead the Church and the people.'

'We educate the children too, in 41,000 local schools. Would you like to hear what I teach the children through our catechism? I ask the questions and they must learn the answers. I ask the question "How should we show our respect for the Tsar?" And they must reply: "We should feel complete loyalty to the Tsar and be prepared to lay down our lives for him. We should without objection fulfil his commands and be obedient to the authorities appointed by him. We should pray for his health and salvation and also for that of all the Ruling Family." Anyone who wants to change this is guilty before God. That is why the Church is in charge of censorship of all books and newspapers.'

You've done some reading up before your trip, and know that not all the people in the Russian Empire are Russians. 'So is everyone a member of the Russian Orthodox Church?' you ask him.

Now he frowns even more. He tells you that on the edges of the Russian Empire there are other faiths. There are Roman Catholics in Poland and even Protestants in the Baltic provinces, and Muslims in the south-east.

'But we are converting more each year to our faith. Soon everyone in Holy Russia will belong to our true Church.'

You seem to have offended him and he now clams up, turning to read his book until he gets off without another word at the next stop.

Middle classes

A small crowd of people get on next. A man sits quietly opposite you, but your attention is taken by a big group, who seem to be all one large family. The men wear cotton turbans on their heads, like peasants do in Turkey, and the women's heads are covered too, with scarves. Their dresses are brightly coloured and they are chattering noisily in a language which is certainly not Russian.

'They are Uzbeks,' says your new neighbour, 'from Tashkent, way down in the south, on the borders of Afghanistan.'

'Are they Russian?'

'They found themselves subjects of the Tsar about 40 years ago when Imperial forces took over their land,' he replies. 'Remember that barely half the people in this empire are Russians. They even have different words: 'Russki' for ethnic Russians and 'Russiski' for non-Russian citizens of the Russian Empire. I am proud to say that I am Polish, but we have been ruled by the Tsars for getting on for 100 years now, since 1815.'

Your new companion is a salesman for a Polish furniture company. He tells you that he sells mainly to middle class people wanting to bring their homes up to date. His trip has not been very successful.

'In Moscow and St Petersburg I can find customers. Bankers and owners of factories who have got money and know what's going on in the rest of the world – more and more of them each year. But out here: nothing much. You know the great Russian writer Gogol? He described the towns as "little dots in an overpowering landscape".'

△ The town of Vitegru.

'What percentage of British people live in towns and cities?' he asks you. 'About 75 per cent by now.'

'Do you know the figure for Russia? Fifteen per cent! Look at these grubby little towns,' he says as the train rattles over a bridge and you both look down on a small town (see the photograph above). 'This is the only town for 40 kilometres in any direction. It's probably got a couple of small factories, a sawmill, a private school, one hotel, some dusty old-fashioned shops and a weekly newspaper. The further east you go, the worse it gets. There'll be a tiny group of educated middle class people: a few lawyers, doctors, teachers, the newspaper editor, forever going the rounds of the same social events. They'll grumble about the backwardness of Russia, the power of the Tsar and the aristocracy, and the ignorance of the peasants, but they do nothing about it.'

He says this lack of a large, well-informed middle class is bad for his business, but then the conversation moves on.

'It's bad for political progress in Russia too. In Britain, your middle classes put pressure on the old system to change and they have had the vote since 1832. Most of your members of parliament are from the middle classes. It's they who have set about improving public health, building hospitals and schools. You have debates in parliament, and plenty of educated people to buy newspapers and join in. Most of your working class have the vote now, I hear, and there is even talk of women voting. Even to suggest such things in Russia can get you into big trouble. No wonder the little middle class groups in the little towns feel isolated and helpless.'

Industrial workers

As your train gets nearer to Moscow, huge factories begin to fill the view and next to them some tall, gloomy buildings like the photograph below. They look rather like army barracks. Your companion puts you right:

'Those are where the workers from that big ironworks live. You'll have heard about our "Great Spurt"?'

◁ Barrack-like blocks like this one were built to house factory workers. Living conditions were cramped, unhygienic and lacking in privacy: these were the conditions which helped to spark the Revolution, as you will see. Russian factories were often very large – the Putilov armaments factory in St Petersburg employed 30,000 workers. This was quite unlike factories in countries like Britain, which had industrialised much earlier. With such rapid expansion, large amounts of accommodation had to be provided as fast as possible for the hundreds of peasants who streamed into the cities to work.

'Yes, the growth rate of your economy is 8 per cent isn't it? Very impressive: highest in Europe!'

'Only because we started from such a low base: 40 per cent of our industries didn't exist ten years ago. But if you start late you can learn from other countries, like you British and the Germans, how to grow fast and make big profits.'

'How do you do that?' you ask.

'Build your factories as large as possible, and get as much out of the workers for as little as possible.'

'And who gets the profits?'

'Lots of our industries are owned by foreign investors, so a lot of the profits don't stay in Russia. Sergei Witte, he's been our Finance Minister since 1894, wanted to industrialise fast. This needed lots of investment, of course. He put up taxes, but also pulled in money from foreign investors, mainly from France, Germany and Britain.'

'So what's it like to work there?'

'Terrible! Our industrial workers are the most wretched people in Russia. They work long hours, for very low pay. Their employers don't care about safety and hideous injuries are common. There's no compensation for accidents, so if you're injured and can't work, that's just your bad luck. The foremen bully the workers – they're even allowed to beat them. And do you know what really hurts? They call them *tyi* (you), but this is the word the masters used to their serfs, instead of *vyi*, which is what free people call each other.

'And then, at the end of the long day, they go back to those blocks we were looking at. They've got no proper lighting, or ventilation, no one has their own room, just a bit curtained off from the rest, so it's dirty and noisy.

'The problem is that many of them are still really peasants. Less than half of our three million workers have actually moved to live in the cities for good. The rest go back to their villages for the harvest and other big events, so they're only lodging in those living blocks.'

'Doesn't the Tsar care about this situation?'

'The Tsar lives in his own world. He likes to think that all Russians are happy, ignorant peasants, devoted to their "Little Father" – that's the tsar – just like in the Middle Ages. It suits him for Russia not to be properly industrialised, for the peasants to just work for a few months in the factories. He thinks they don't need **trade unions** with their "Little Father" to look after them!

'I'll tell you this, my friend: it can't last. Full-time industrial workers may be only 5 per cent of the population but they're increasing fast. They're not stupid: they talk, they get themselves organised. There are strikes – more every year. More and more of them are leaving the village completely – the permanent population of our cities has doubled in size since 1860. Many of these industrial workers are getting educated. If anything is going to change Russia, it'll come from the factories and the cities. We in the Social Democratic Workers Party…'

Then he stopped, fearing that he'd said too much. You assure him his views are safe with you, but he's relieved that you've nearly reached the Yaroslavsky Station, in Moscow, the terminus of the Trans-Siberian Railway, where everyone gets off.

You are going on the overnight train to St Petersburg, so enjoy a ten-minute walk across Kalanchyovskaya Square to the Petersburg Station and your sleeping berth for the overnight journey. Next morning in St Petersburg, feeling stiff from your days stuck on the train, you decide to leave your luggage and go for a stroll. The station leads straight out on to the Nevsky Prospekt, the most important street in St Petersburg (see the photograph opposite). It all seems much more familiar than anything you've seen in the last few days: European goods in the busy and well-stocked shops, horse-drawn cabs, restaurants and cafés, trams, fashionably-dressed men and women, who could just as easily be walking down Piccadilly, or the Champs Elysées in Paris.

Only the lettering on the shop fronts, the voices you can hear and some of the clothing tell you that you are still in Russia.

Trade unions
In many countries at this time, workers in the same industry banded together in trade unions in order to put collective pressure on employers to deal with their grievances.

△ The Nevsky Prospekt in St Petersburg runs in a straight line across the city. In this hand-coloured postcard from about 1900 you can see a horse-drawn tram, cabs and private carriages. There are wide pavements for window-shopping. This street was to become the scene of many demonstrations in the revolutions of 1905 and 1917.

■ Your journey is over, and you've seen how different Russia is from Britain. You've also seen some of the huge contrasts in the country, from illiterate peasants living beyond the Ural Mountains, to the sophisticates of the streets of St Petersburg.

Look back over all the people you have met on this journey.

- What are their hopes and fears?

- Does it seem likely that their hopes can be met, and their fears set aside, as Russia moves into the twentieth century?

- What obstacles might there be to achieving their hopes?

- Some historians have argued that it is Russia's geography which has determined its history. They would say that Russia is too big and too poor to rule except by brutal force. As you read through this book, think about how far you agree.

2 The Russian Revolution: The essentials

In the early years of the twentieth century, Russia had not one but three revolutions. The first was in 1905, both of the others in 1917. Here are two photographs from before (1), and after (2), the 1917 Russian Revolutions.

Photograph 1 was taken in early 1914. It shows dinner at a ball given by Countess Shuvalov in her luxurious palace in St Petersburg. At the ball the lights glittered on the glasses of wine, the lavish flowers, the women in chic dresses and fashionable hair styles, the men in crisp uniforms and evening dress. These were the nobility of Tsarist Russia, displaying their wealth and power. They and their families had always ruled Russia. The men here were the only ones with access to all the top jobs. They owned town houses in St Petersburg and Moscow, and huge country estates.

Before this year was half over, more than a million angry and desperate Russian workers had been involved in strikes.

(1) Before

Photograph 2 was taken in 1918. It shows ex-officers of the Tsar's army being made to clear the street at a market in Petrograd, as St Petersburg was now called. They are under orders from a Soviet Commissar (on the left in high boots) accompanied by guards. Only members of the privileged upper classes could become officers in the Tsar's army. We don't know if the ex-officers bent over their shovels in Photograph 2 were at the ball in Photograph 1, but clearly something dramatic has happened in Russia in only four years. Indeed, the lives of all the people in both photographs were totally changed by the revolution.

(2) After

Why is the Russian Revolution worth studying?

- It's got all the elements of a great story. The setting is exotic. The action is often violent. The characters are colourful.
- Historians try to provide explanations of big events. Why do things happen? Did the Revolution happen because of one or two key individuals? Or the actions of the unknown and unnamed masses of people? Was it inevitable? Or just a combination of accidents? By the time you've finished you'll have developed your own ideas about what a revolution is, and why this one happened, which you can apply to other historical events you may study.
- 'Tell me what you think of the Russian Revolution and I'll tell you who you are!' Ever since 1917 the Russian Revolution has been studied by anyone interested in politics. Everyone who has written about it has a point of view, usually a political point of view. 'Neutral' history is an impossibility: after all, no one writes history from a desk on a desert island.
- You'll find that these interpretations have changed over time. So, by making up your mind about what you think about the Russian Revolution, you'll find out something about yourself, too.

A chronological overview of the Russian Revolution

The point of this timeline is so that you can see the whole picture before you start. The individual enquiries in this book will take you through the details, but this spread is your 'satnav across time', so you can see where you're going.

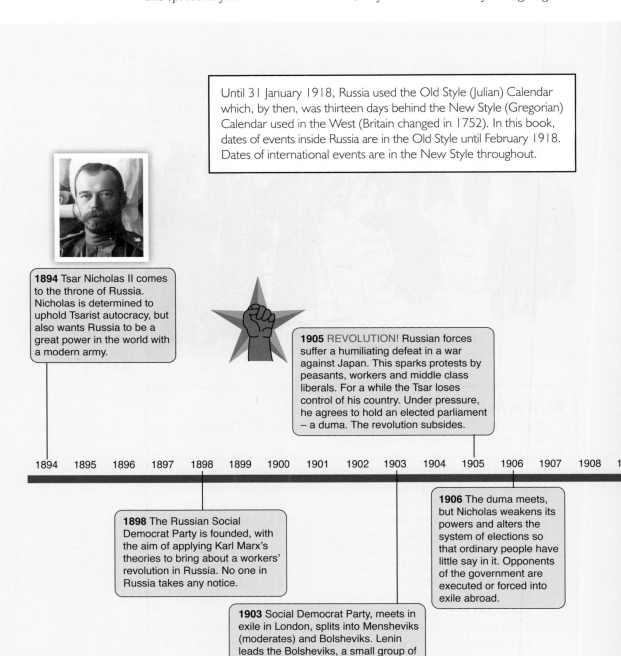

Until 31 January 1918, Russia used the Old Style (Julian) Calendar which, by then, was thirteen days behind the New Style (Gregorian) Calendar used in the West (Britain changed in 1752). In this book, dates of events inside Russia are in the Old Style until February 1918. Dates of international events are in the New Style throughout.

1894 Tsar Nicholas II comes to the throne of Russia. Nicholas is determined to uphold Tsarist autocracy, but also wants Russia to be a great power in the world with a modern army.

1905 REVOLUTION! Russian forces suffer a humiliating defeat in a war against Japan. This sparks protests by peasants, workers and middle class liberals. For a while the Tsar loses control of his country. Under pressure, he agrees to hold an elected parliament – a duma. The revolution subsides.

1894 1895 1896 1897 1898 1899 1900 1901 1902 1903 1904 1905 1906 1907 1908 19

1898 The Russian Social Democrat Party is founded, with the aim of applying Karl Marx's theories to bring about a workers' revolution in Russia. No one in Russia takes any notice.

1906 The duma meets, but Nicholas weakens its powers and alters the system of elections so that ordinary people have little say in it. Opponents of the government are executed or forced into exile abroad.

1903 Social Democrat Party, meets in exile in London, splits into Mensheviks (moderates) and Bolsheviks. Lenin leads the Bolsheviks, a small group of dedicated revolutionaries. No one in Russia takes any notice.

■ Just reading this spread isn't enough to understand it. You need to transfer this information into your own way of telling the story.

The boxes with information about what happened at each date are placed **according to how successful the revolutionaries were** – the higher up the page, the more successful. Using this timeline, talk about:

1 when the greatest changes happened

2 the patterns of change.

January 1918 Bolsheviks exclude all other parties from power – one party rule.
March 1918 Peace with Germany at the Treaty of Brest Litovsk.
May 1918 Communists hold less than half of Russia and Civil War breaks out with their many opponents. The Bolsheviks change their name to the Communist Party.
July 1918 Tsar Nicholas II and all his family are executed.

October 1917 REVOLUTION! Bolsheviks seize power. Lenin is the ruler of Russia.

December 1917 Bolshevik government takes over all banks, businesses and trade. The Cheka is formed and uses terror against Bolsheviks' enemies.

February 1917 REVOLUTION! Massive protests on the streets. Soldiers fraternise with the demonstrators. Nicholas abdicates. A Provisional Government is formed, promises to carry out reforms and hold proper democratic elections later, but in the meantime to carry on the war.

April 1917 Lenin returns to Russia and calls for peace, land reform and revolution.

July 1917 Kerensky takes over as Prime Minister of the Provisional Government. By September Growing dissatisfaction with the Provisional Government. Increasing numbers of people turning to the Bolsheviks.

1918–21 Ferocious Civil War. The Communists ('Reds') are eventually victorious, but Russia is in ruins. The New Economic Policy is introduced, allowing private trade again. Some economic recovery follows.

1914–17 Russia fights in the First World War on the side of the Allies. Defeats and incompetent organisation bring many casualties. Russian economy begins to crumble under the pressure of the war and food shortages.

010   1911   1917   1918   1919   1920   1921   1922   1923   1924

1911 Stolypin is assassinated. He had carried out radical reforms, trying to turn the peasants into small capitalist farmers. After his death his reforms languish.

1924 Lenin dies after suffering from a series of severe strokes in 1922.

Finding patterns in history: Karl Marx

Obviously history never repeats itself exactly, but do you think there are patterns across similar events? Karl Marx thought that there were. His ideas had an enormous influence on the Russian Revolution, both in causing it and explaining it afterwards. Before beginning to study the Revolution it is vital to have an understanding of what he said.

Marx wanted to give history the status of a science, so he looked for patterns in the past. He was so certain that he had found them that he called them 'laws':

1. There are five stages in human history (see the diagram on page 21).
2. At each stage in history, political power lies with whoever has economic power. That is, control of how the things everyone needs – food, for example – are produced and sold.
3. The class which wields this economic power prospers by exploiting the classes who do not. Eventually the exploited class turns on the exploiters and forces the system to change, and so human history progresses to the next stage. This change might be gradual, or violent – a revolution. All history is the story of these class struggles.

△ Karl Marx (1818–83) was a German economist, historian, writer and revolutionary. He came from a comfortably off family and went to Berlin University, after which he made a precarious living as a journalist and political agitator in Germany, France and Belgium. Following the failure of the 1848 revolutions in Germany and France, Marx fled to London, where he lived for the rest of his life. Most of his research was carried out in the Reading Room of the British Museum and his major work, *Das Kapital*, was published in 1867.

Marx said that western Europe had just moved into Stage 4 (see the diagram). In this stage, those who own businesses ('**bourgeois capitalists**') get rich by extracting as much work for as little pay from the workers ('**proletariat**') as they can. Eventually the workers will rise up in a proletarian revolution and force another change. *'The bourgeoisie produces its own grave-diggers. Its fall and the victory of the proletariat are inevitable'* (from *The Communist Manifesto*, 1848).

Marx's assertion that revolution was inevitable had an enormous impact, and nowhere more than in Russia. His explanation of the processes of change seemed to fit their history. But what should people wanting radical changes do? Wait for the unfairness of capitalism to move Russia on, as Marx insisted it surely would? Or give the forces of history a push, by becoming a revolutionary agitator? So the arguments raged.

Then, after the Russian Revolutions, more argument raged over what exactly had happened. Did events in Russia prove that Marx was right, as some historians tried to show? Or did the way things panned out in Russia prove that he was completely wrong, and there are no laws of history, as other historians said. That argument is still going on, and you are hereby invited to take part!

The next spread introduces the main arguments, and you will be able to follow these arguments through the enquiries in this book.

Karl Marx's five stages of history

Stage 1: Primitive communism
Pre-historic people live as hunters in small groups. No one exploits anyone else and everyone is roughly equal.

Stage 2: Slavery
Great warrior-kings in ancient Babylon, Egypt and Rome lived well by exploiting the work of masses of slaves.

Stage 3: Feudalism
The monarch (king, Tsar) and a small number of landowning nobles, live well by exploiting the peasants, who work the land.

Bourgeois revolution
Middle class merchants and industrialists ('bourgeois capitalists') want the country to be run to benefit business, not agriculture. They seize power from the monarch and nobles.

Stage 4: Capitalism
After the bourgeois revolution the means of production (factories, mines, banks, etc.) are run by private enterprise. That is, they are owned by bourgeois capitalists who invest money in them and want a good profit. They achieve this by exploiting the industrial workers – the proletariat. There is democratic government, but although lots of people may have the right to vote, the bourgeoisie run the country.

Proletarian revolution
The workers rise up in revolution and throw out their bourgeois masters:
'Workers of the world unite!
You have nothing to lose but your chains!'

Stage 5: The Workers' State
Socialism, or communism. This will be the final, perfect stage of human history. Everyone is equal and no one exploits anyone else. People work according to their ability and the state rewards them according to what they need.

How do historians explain the Russian Revolution?

Most people probably expect a historian to deliver **'the truth'** about the past. I think the really interesting thing about the Russian Revolution is that its historians have come from different standpoints and so produce quite different explanations of what was happening. Here are three typical standpoints from historians of the Revolution.

Overview
Bolsheviks, directed by Lenin's genius, led the Revolution.

The Soviet view

From soon after the Revolution the Communists wrote their own version of events. The 'Commission on the History of the Russian Communist Party and the October Revolution' was set up in 1920 and linked the story of the Revolution with the story of the Communist Party. They described how the Revolution followed Karl Marx's theory. Lenin and the Bolshevik Party provided leadership for the uprising of the workers against their masters who were exploiting their labour. With the 'cult' of Lenin after his death in 1924, all Soviet explanations of the Revolution centred around him. These kinds of explanations of the Revolution dominated Russian historical writing until the fall of the Soviet Union in 1989.

Overview
The October Revolution was a Communist seizure of power; the people were manipulated by evil Lenin.

The western liberal view

Western countries hated and feared Communist Russia from the start. This intensified during the Cold War after 1945. Western liberal historians mainly drew their evidence from Russians who had fled from Communist Russia. These witnesses were, of course, hostile to Communism and thus to the Soviet view of the Revolution. Western liberal writers sought to show that the October Revolution was an illegal seizure of power, a mere *coup d'état*. The Communist governments which followed on from 1917 were therefore seen as illegitimate and should be overthrown.

Western liberal historians did not accept the Marxist view of history. They argued that the Revolution was the result of a combination of circumstances. However, they did agree on the important role of Lenin, not as a hero, but as an unscrupulous operator who manipulated events to gain power.

Overview
The Revolutions were popular uprisings; they were not controlled by the Bolsheviks.

Red Guards
Armed Bolshevik militia, active in Petrograd in October 1917

The New Left revisionist view

From the 1970s younger historians began to focus their research on social history. This led them to the study of individual factories, villages, **Red Guards** and army units to find out what was actually going on at grass roots level. Their research led New Left historians to criticise both Soviet and western liberal interpretations. They suggested that the Revolutions arose from genuine grievances felt by ordinary Russian people. Studies of their protests and how they were expressed put the Revolutions in a new perspective. They were not part of a Marxist law, nor were they told what to think by the Bolsheviks. But they were not the mindless violent mob, manipulated by Lenin, which western liberal historians described, either.

Isaak Mints

Isaak Mints (1896–1991) joined the Bolshevik Party in 1917, began his historical research in the 1920s and was head of the History Department at Moscow University from 1932 to 1949. His services to Soviet history brought him many honours, including the Lenin Prize and, in 1976, Hero of Soviet Labour. He chaired the group of historians whose task was to write the History of the October Revolution for its fiftieth anniversary 'under the direct guidance of the **Politburo**'. The three volume history explains the central role of the Bolshevik Party, not only in the October Revolution, but the February Revolution too. Other parties are summarily dismissed as 'petty bourgeois'. Trotsky (see pages 114–115) is hardly mentioned, but Lenin is the hero, named on a quarter of all the pages.

Politburo
Central Committee of the Communist Party and so the ruling body of the Soviet Union

Richard Pipes

Richard Pipes was born into a successful Polish Jewish family in 1923. He and his family fled from the Nazis to the USA in 1940. He became a US citizen and taught at Harvard University from 1950 to 1996. In his writing on Russian history, he emphasises the autocratic nature of Russian rulers right back to the fifteenth century. He is a savage critic of Lenin. In his view, the October Revolution was a disaster, in which a tiny handful of intellectuals took power in a coup and established a repressive government. To Pipes, Nazi Germany and Communist Russia were similar, both being totalitarian regimes bent on world domination. His anti-Communist views brought him to the attention of the US government and he was made a member of the National Security Council, the President's main advisory body on foreign affairs, from 1981–82.

Steven A Smith

Some idea of how Revisionist historians changed the two orthodoxies which had dominated writing about the Russian Revolution can be seen in this quotation from the British historian Steven A Smith. Smith, now Professor of History at Essex University, researched the beliefs and actions of factory workers in Petrograd. Writing in 1987, in an essay entitled *'Petrograd in 1917 – The view from below'*, he says:

'To be sure, Bolshevik agitation and organisation played a crucial role in radicalising the masses. But the Bolsheviks themselves did not create popular discontent and revolutionary feelings. This grew out of the masses' own experience of complex economic and social upheaval and political events.'

How did the Tsars rule Russia?

The last Tsar of Russia was Nicholas II. He nearly lost his throne in 1905, was thrown out in 1917 and murdered in 1918. One of the questions you will be bound to think about as you read this book is whether history is made by single, named individuals, or by the unnamed masses of the people. Hundreds of thousands of people made personal decisions to get involved in the Russian revolutions, so it must seem extraordinary to be looking at this one person.

But a Tsar of Russia was in an extraordinary position for a twentieth century ruler: he was an **autocrat**. That is, he had unrestricted power over his country. There was no parliament, no supreme court to question his decisions. He had advisers, the Imperial Council, but he could ignore what they told him. He had ministers, but he appointed them and dismissed them as he wished and they rarely met together. As Tsarism's greatest supporter, the Russian Orthodox Church (of which the Tsar was the head) put it: he was responsible only to God. In this situation the personality and actions of this one man became very important.

The decisions taken by Nicholas' predecessors as Tsar, his grandfather and his father, therefore had a great impact on the people of Russia and on the situation Nicholas inherited.

autocrat
A ruler with absolute power, whose word is law and who does not have to share power

The Tsars' dilemma

Option 1	OR	Option 2
Should Russia modernise its economy and reform its government, becoming a democratic industrial Great Power – a bit like Britain, for example?		Should Russia stay different, resist calls for change, remain a nation of what the Tsars saw as happy peasants watched over by their 'Little Father', the Tsar?

Under the tsarist system only the Tsar himself could resolve this dilemma. What choices had Nicholas' predecessors taken?

Alexander II, Tsar 1855–81: reform and retreat

Alexander II was Nicholas II's grandfather. He came to the throne just as Russia was badly defeated in the Crimean War. The Russian army was seen to be badly equipped and badly led, its illiterate serf conscripts incapable of becoming a modern army. Voices on all sides called for reform and for a while Alexander II listened to them and took the reform route.

- He freed the serfs (some books will call this the '**emancipation** of the serfs), in 1861.
- He set up the *zemstva*, elected local councils.
- He reformed the law courts, and cut back on censorship.
- He reformed the army, introducing modern weapons and training for officers.
- More universities and schools were started. Schools were taken out of the hands of the Church and handed over to the *zemstva* to run.

Emancipation
Before 1861 most Russian peasants were serfs, unfree, owned by their lord. After Alexander II's emancipation they became free peasants, but were still tied to the village by annual payments they had to make for the land they received (see also page 34).

Alexander, however, was not a convinced reformer. When a revolutionary tried to assassinate him in 1865 Alexander back-tracked. His reforming ministers were dismissed and replaced by **reactionaries**: censorship increased, opponents were arrested and many died in prison. Dangerous subjects like history and science were banned from universities. All this did Alexander himself no good: the revolutionaries got him in the end. He was killed by a bomb thrown by a member of 'People's Will' (see page 43) in 1881.

(see page 43)

reactionary
Someone opposed to all change, who believes that any change is a change for the worse, that the old ways of doing things are the best

Insight

Alexander III, Tsar 1881–94: reaction takes over

Alexander III was Nicholas II's father. He was a big, physically strong man, who had spent his life in the army. He had opposed all his father's reforms and Alexander II's assassination only confirmed to him that he was right. He made it clear as soon as he became Tsar that he intended to preserve autocracy and suppress all opposition. But he wanted the best of both worlds: holding fast to autocracy, but also encouraging economic modernisation – because only a modern economy could support Russian ambitions to remain a Great Power in the world, with a modern army and navy.

Therefore many of Alexander II's reforms were reversed, or watered down.

- Only the children of the rich and the upper classes were allowed into the schools which prepared students for university.
- Women were barred from universities.
- Censorship increased. Many newspapers were banned. It became a criminal offence to criticise the Tsar.
- He began a policy of 'Russification'; that is the Russian language, Russian Orthodox religion and customs were promoted. Other languages, religions and ethnic groups were discriminated against.
- He set up the *Okhrana*, the secret police. The *Okhrana* spied on opposition groups, and arrested thousands of their supporters. Many were executed, or exiled to Siberia. Opposition groups were crushed, or went abroad.
- 1890 *Zemstvo* Act restricted voting in elections to the *zemstvo* councils, so fewer peasants and non-nobles were elected. Provincial governors appointed by the Tsar were given powers to overrule *zemstvo* decisions. If there was trouble in an area, the whole province could be put under military rule.
- Land Captains, appointed by the provincial governors, had powers to overrule peasant decision-making in the *mir* (village).

Nikita Khrushchev, leader of the Soviet Union, 1953–64, said: 'Historians are dangerous people – they can upset people.' Why are historians dangerous people?

△ Tsar Alexander III.

The situation Nicholas inherited in 1894

Neither Nicholas' father nor grandfather made clear decisions as to which way Russia should go. The result was that by 1894, tsarist Russia was already under strain. Some aspects such as the economy was modernising fast (you can read more about this in Chapter 3), but this had not been accompanied by any moves towards real democracy. The economic reforms were creating massive new cities, and a new class in Russia – industrial workers. The old Russian society made up entirely of peasants was gradually disappearing.

Tsar Nicholas II: the man, his personality and his family (1)

Summing up a human being is an almost impossible task – try it on your friends! It's even harder when that person has been dead for nearly 100 years. So here is some evidence: stories, pictures, his own words and those of his contemporaries and subsequent historians about the last tsar of Russia, Nicholas II. Solving Russia's problems was going to need a strong and thoughtful leader, capable of taking advice, then making decisions and sticking to them: how suitable does Nicholas appear to have been for this task?

What is going to happen to me and to all of Russia? I am not prepared to be a Tsar. I never wanted to become one. I know nothing of the business of ruling. I have no idea how to talk to ministers.

(Nicholas' words on being told of the unexpected death of his father in 1894)

Through his education Nicholas had all the talents and charms of an English public schoolboy. He spoke English like an Oxford professor and French and German well. His manners were impeccable. But of the practical knowledge required to run a country the size of Russia – and a country in a pre-revolutionary situation – Nicholas possessed almost nothing … When Pobedonostsev tried to instruct him in the workings of the state, he became 'actively absorbed in picking his nose'.

(Orlando Figes, British historian, 1996)

[Nicholas is] the father of his people, over whose needs he keeps an earnest and compassionate watch. [He devotes] special care and attention to the welfare and moral development [of the peasants, whose huts he frequently entered] to see how they live and partake of their milk and black bread … Thousands of invisible threads centre in the Tsar's heart, and these threads stretch to the huts of the poor and the palaces of the rich. And that is the reason the Russian people always acclaims its Tsar with such fervent enthusiasm, whether in St Petersburg … or in the towns and villages.

(Nicholas' official biographer, 1913)

△ In 1913 there were celebrations of 300 years of rule by Romanov tsars. These historic roots were very important to Nicholas and this picture shows him dressed as Tsar of Muscovy from 1613. *Does this look like a picture of a twentieth-century ruler?*

A few days after Nicholas' coronation in 1896 a fair was held just outside Moscow. A huge crowd gathered, expecting to receive traditional gifts of tankards and special biscuits and enjoy free beer and sausages. For some reason the crowd panicked and in the rush 1400 people were trampled to death and 600 injured. Nicholas continued with the celebrations, attending a ball given by the French Ambassador that evening and other events in the next few days. An enquiry revealed that Grand Duke Sergius, Nicholas' brother-in-law, was responsible for the organisation of the fair, but this was hushed up.

△ Nicholas, his wife, Alexandra, daughters and son around 1910.

He was certainly no dimmer than his look-alike cousin, George V, who was a model of a **constitutional king**. *Nicholas was mild-mannered, with an excellent memory and sense of decorum, all of which would have made him ideal for the largely ceremonial tasks of a constitutional monarch. But Nicholas was Emperor and Autocrat of All the Russias.*

(The historian Orlando Figes discusses whether Nicholas was intelligent and compares him to the British King George V, 1910–36)

His apparently diplomatic handling of his advisers, whereby he seemed to take their views into account, obscured what was in fact the Tsar's dislike of argument or discord … His government lacked co-ordination, coherence, consistency or a grand plan. One of the potential benefits of autocratic rule was a clear and well-directed policy, yet this was flagrantly lacking …

(Sarah Badcock, in *Essays in honour of R B McKean*, 2005)

constitutional king
A monarch whose power is restricted by a democratic constitution, unlike Nicholas, whose powers were limitless

Nicholas did not have secretaries. He did all his own filing, licked and addressed his own envelopes. He did not have close personal advisers who could have helped him develop his own ideas.

Nicholas married one of his cousins, Princess Alexandra. She was the grand-daughter of Queen Victoria, born in Germany, but had lived in England from the age of six, when her mother died. She and Nicholas spoke to each other in English: 'hubby' and 'wifey' were their affectionate names for each other. Becoming Empress aged only 22, she took on the autocratic role surprisingly quickly. When Victoria wrote to her, advising her to work to earn her subjects' respect, she replied:

You are mistaken, my dear grandmama; Russia is not England. Here we do not need to earn the love of the people. The Russian people revere their Tsars as divine beings … As far as St Petersburg society is concerned, that is something which one may wholly disregard. The opinions of those who make up this society … have no significance whatsoever.

This last remark made her extremely unpopular at court, of course, and she was rarely seen in public. That did not mean she stayed out of politics. In private she bossed Nicholas about, ordering him to switch policies and ministers as her whims took her. 'Be more autocratic than Peter the Great, and sterner than Ivan the Terrible,' she told him.

◁ A tragedy in their family life increased Nicholas and Alexandra's closeness and mutual dependency. The pressure is always on a royal consort to produce a son to carry on the succession. After giving birth to four daughters, a son, Alexei, was born in 1904. Unfortunately he suffered from haemophilia. This is a blood condition in which the slightest knock can cause internal bleeding, perhaps fatally. Alexei was unable to lead a normal life and was guarded, and often carried, by a sailor, Derevenko, as you can see here. Haemophilia is hereditary, carried through Alexandra's genes, as she knew. She came to believe only a miracle could cure him, and turned to religion.

In 2000, after some 8 years of study, the council of Bishops of the Russian Orthodox Church voted unanimously to recognise Nicholas, Alexandra and their five children as saints.

(From the website: OrthodoxWiki, 'a free-content encyclopedia and information center for Orthodox Christianity')

People do not influence events. God directs everything and the Tsar, as God's anointed, should not take advice from anyone but only follow his divine inspiration.

(Nicholas II)

We talked for two solid hours. He shook my hand. He embraced me. He wished me all the luck in the world. I returned home beside myself with happiness … and found a written order for my dismissal on my desk.

(Witte describes his dismissal after eleven years as Finance Minister)

△ This statue, put up in 1909, shows a massive Tsar Alexander sitting squarely astride an enormous standing horse. It looks as if the horse and rider will never move, and for many this symbolised the rule of the tsars: solid, rigid, heavy, unable to move. Nicholas commissioned this statue of his father himself and was very pleased with it – which tells us something about him.

Workers called it 'the Hippopotamus' and recited the verse (which rhymes in Russian):

Here stands a chest of drawers,

On the chest, a hippopotamus,

And on the hippopotamus sits an idiot.

3 Was Tsar Nicholas II mainly to blame for the 1905 Revolution?

△ **Was this the moment when Tsar Nicholas II lost the unquestioning obedience of his people?**

icon
An icon is a religious painting. Icons were regarded as holy objects, were kissed or bowed to in church and carried in religious processions

9 January 1905 was a sunny Sunday in St Petersburg. A procession of workers (men, women and children) in their best clothes and carrying holy **icons**, headed across the ice to the Tsar's Winter Palace. They were mainly workers who were on strike from the huge Putilov arms factory. Led by a priest, Father Gapon, they carried a petition to the Tsar listing their grievances, believing that as their 'Holy Father', he would listen and put things right. They were met by soldiers with rifles. The photograph shows what happened next. After two warning shots, they fired into the crowd. 200 people were killed and 800 wounded. The day became known as Bloody Sunday.

Over the next few months of 1905 there were more demonstrations, strikes in the factories and mutinies in the armed forces. Peasants all over Russia burnt the grand houses of the landowners. Non-Russian parts of the Empire declared independence. By October Nicholas was no longer in control of his country and was forced to promise to rule more democratically. This concession was just enough and the Tsar survived (as you will see in Chapter 4) – the 1905 Revolution failed to remove him. But Russia was never to be the same afterwards.

Enquiry Focus: Was Tsar Nicholas II mainly to blame for the 1905 Revolution?

Each chapter of this book focuses on an enquiry: that is, the pathway you use to get into each topic is indicated by a question, a problem needing an answer. This is just how historians work, and it means that you have to read the pages which follow with a purpose. So, DON'T just start reading and making notes, pushing the question to the back of your mind. That way you end with lots of notes, but no answers. DO think about the question as you read and gradually put together your response.

We'll always begin by looking carefully at the question. This enquiry is a kind of explanation question exploring the reasons why there was a revolution in Russia in 1905 and how far Tsar Nicholas II was to blame.

A key word in the question is 'mainly': do **most** of the causes lead back to Nicholas? That is the suggestion, the hypothesis which the question is asking you to examine and to judge whether it is true or not.

1 Your initial thoughts. Think back to the people on the long train journey you read about on pages 4–15. In 1905, people from several of these groups rose up in protest. What could have driven each of them to revolution? And do their motives all lead back to Nicholas?

2 To keep track of the overall answer we're going to use the **causation map** below. Pages 32–45

discuss the factors shown in the causation map. When you've read each factor:

a) make short notes explaining how the factor contributed to the outbreak of the 1905 revolution

b) decide to what extent Nicholas was to blame for the factor and annotate your causation map as follows:

- if Nicholas was completely or mostly to blame add a large red N by the factor
- if Nicholas was partly to blame add a smaller blue N by the factor
- if Nicholas was not to blame at all then do NOT put an N by the factor.

For example, Nicholas was not to blame for poor harvests of 1902 and 1903 so you would not add an N by the bad harvests factor, number 3 on the map.

As you read the chapter and annotate the causation map you will be able to see how important Nicholas was in the outbreak of the revolution. If there are mainly red Ns then he was mainly to blame but if there are lots of blue Ns and blanks then the hypothesis is not true.

At the end of the enquiry you will be prompted to revise your hypothesis and finalise your answer.

1 The repressive Tsarist system
2 Peasants' anger
9 Defeat in war with Japan 1904–05
3 Bad harvests 1902 and 1903
The 1905 Revolution
8 Opposition groups: a) Liberal reformists b) Revolutionaries
4 Workers' anger
7 Middle classes' resentment
6 National and ethnic minorities' anger
5 World trade recession from 1900

The repressive Tsarist system

As you have discovered from pages 26–29, Nicholas was clearly not a strong leader. He was not likely to use his power to lead the country in his own direction. He was heavily influenced by the policies of his father and grandfather and, in the first part of his reign, by two powerful ministers, both inherited from his father.

△ Konstantin Pobedonostsev (1827–1907).

△ Sergei Witte (1849–1915).

arch-reactionary
Someone vehemently opposed to all change

Pobedonostsev was a brilliant lawyer and **arch-reactionary**. His pale, gaunt figure and unrelenting views, powerfully expressed, struck fear into anyone who suggested reform. A member of the Tsar's Council for twenty years, he was adviser to Alexander II and Alexander III. Alexander III also made him Nicholas' tutor. We can only imagine the effect this imposing, deeply serious, elderly man had on young Nicholas. Pobedonostsev believed that Russia was 'different' and needed to be ruled differently. Russians needed a strong, fatherly autocracy: parliamentary government was 'un-Russian'. He was opposed to western European ideas such as trial by jury and freedom of the press. As chief minister for the Russian Orthodox Church, he was largely responsible for the policy of Russification (see page 39). Anti-Semitism increased, with his encouragement.

The other leading minister was Sergei Witte who, from the 1890s, directed Russia in a process of industrialisation which transformed the country's industries (see pages 36–38). Witte's origins tell you something about the internationalism of the Russian Empire: his father was German–Dutch, his mother was Russian and he was brought up in Tbilisi, Georgia, then a province of Russia. He became an expert on railways and finance and served Alexander III and Nicholas II as Minister of Finance 1892–1903, chairman of the Committee of Ministers (as near as Tsars got to a Prime Minister) 1903–06. He was happy to work for the Tsars because, in an autocracy, things can get done more quickly, more consistently, without the bother of elections, or criticism by a free press.

It is an indicator of how Nicholas and his predecessors worked, and their inconsistent direction, that Witte and Pobedonostsev were both ministers at the same time. They were different in so many ways: Witte had none of Pobedonostsev's nationalistic views. He worked easily with Jews (his second wife was a converted Jew) and other non-Russians, and in 1905 recommended that Nicholas set up an elected parliament. While Pobedonostsev wanted to preserve an older, peasant Russia, Witte ignored the peasants.

Back on page 24, we looked at the two choices facing the last Tsars:

Option I	OR Option 2
Should Russia modernise its economy and reform its government, becoming a democratic industrial Great Power – a bit like Britain, for example?	Should Russia stay different, resist calls for change, remain a nation of what the Tsars saw as happy peasants watched over by their 'Little Father', the Tsar?

After his early reforming period ended sharply in 1865, Alexander II plumped for Option 2 – Russia was going to stay an autocracy, and a repressive one too.

Alexander III followed the same road – politically at least. However, at the same time he appointed and encouraged Witte's industrialisation programme. He wanted the best of both options: a modernised industrial economy, but no democracy.

Nicholas, bullied by his father and tutored by Pobedonostsev, was always likely to do the same. This increased the likelihood that anyone who wanted to get rid of a repressive autocracy would have to do so through revolution. The only person who could have changed the direction Russia was going was Nicholas. He could, for example, have dismissed Pobedonostsev, and dealt with the social strains caused by Witte's rapid industrialisation. But he didn't, and so must carry responsibility for the problems his ministers' policies brought about.

Factor 1

1 How would you apportion blame for the repressive autocratic Tsarist system? Was it Nicholas' inheritance, so the blame passes to his predecessors? If you agree with this judgement, you need to place a small 'N', or none at all on the causation map. Or does he carry the blame for failing to modernise an antiquated system? If you think this, then you will place a large 'N' on the causation map.

2 Annotate your causation map and then write a few sentences explaining your decision.

△ A photograph from the 1890s of a peasant family in central Russia.

See also pages 5–7 for further discussion of the peasants' problems.

The peasants – poverty and anger

Alexander II's emancipation (freeing) of the serfs in 1861 (see page 24) turned them into free peasants. No longer could they be bought and sold by their owners. Emancipation was carried out with high hopes: the government expected agricultural productivity to increase and that the sale of farm products abroad would fund investment in industry. It didn't happen for two main reasons.

Firstly, peasant farming methods were backward and largely unchanging. They cultivated the land in strips scattered across the fields, just like in medieval England. The distribution of land was decided by the *mir*, the village council, dominated by the village elders, committed to doing things the same way they always had been. Most peasants were illiterate, so it was difficult to persuade them to change their ways, for example to introduce new crops, or fertilisers, or crop rotations. Productivity in 1900 was about a quarter of what it was in Britain. Natural disasters in an area could cause crop failure and hunger: 400,000 died of famine in the Volga region in 1891–92.

A second reason for the failure to modernise, and the source of much peasant anger, was that most were in dire poverty. When they were emancipated, they had to pay for the land they received over 49 years. The price was set too high and by 1900 peasant debts exceeded the amount they were paying back. The result was that they were tied to the land by their debts, unable to leave. Added to this, Witte raised taxes to pay for his industrialisation programme. Although the peasants were almost self-sufficient, they found themselves having to pay more for basic items such as oil for lighting, sugar, matches and vodka.

Their poverty was also increased by the custom of the *mir* that every son of a peasant was entitled to some land in the village. This meant that the available land was divided and sub-divided and, with a rising population, this meant that each peasant family had less and less to live on. The government calculated that a family needed **5.5 hectares** of land to survive; by 1900 22 per cent of peasants farmed less than this. Locked into poverty, the peasants cast angry and envious eyes on the big estates still owned by the landlords and violent attacks on landowners' property became common. In 1898 a government report noted:

> … peasant disorders in the form of systematic damage to landowners' fields and meadows, driving away cattle under the protection of men armed with sticks, staves and pitchforks.

Bad harvests in 1902 and 1903 also brought an increase in the number of outbreaks of violence and calls from landlords for military protection. Nicholas was disinclined to make any changes to the lives of the peasants, about whom he had an entirely unrealistic, sentimental view (see page 26).

5.5 hectares of land is almost the area of five football pitches.

Factor 2

1 Why was anger increasing among peasants in the years before 1905?

2 To what extent was Nicholas responsible for their poverty and anger? Now continue Activity 2b on page 31, annotating your causation map with large 'N', small 'N', or none at all, depending on your decision.

Variety and generalisation

In order to say anything sensible about large groups of people, historians have to generalise. For example, this section is about 'the peasants'. There were over 100 million of these in Russia in 1900. The historian Christopher Read points out that: *'The Russian Empire … had the cultural variety of the British Empire all wrapped into one vast land-mass which covered one-sixth of the land area of the globe.'* He goes on to describe some of the more exotic inhabitants of the Russian Empire, from reindeer herdsmen in Lapland in the north, to mountain shepherds in the Caucasus to the south, from nomadic Buddhists in the far east to poor Jewish *shtetls* (villages) in the west.

Even if we just take central Russia and the Ukraine, where 66 per cent of Russian peasants lived, there was variety. In the south, just north of the Black Sea, landowners and peasants were successfully producing grain to sell to the growing cities. Slightly further north was the Black Earth belt which ran right across Russia from Romania to the Urals. The land here was fertile, hence its name, but in the process of emancipation, landlords had taken plenty of the best land. A high and rising population meant that this was an area of rural poverty, resentment and hunger for land. In the provinces around the Baltic (later to become independent Lithuania, Latvia and Estonia), German and Swedish landowners ran prosperous farms, employing peasants as wage-labourers on low pay. In Siberia, on the other hand, there were few noble landlords, and peasants ran their farms themselves.

Obviously, we can't review all these regional differences all the time. We have to make generalisations about 'the peasants'. But these variations do present problems for historians of Russian history and you need to take them into account in the kind of language you use.

Anger amongst industrial workers

From the 1890s **Sergei Witte** directed a process of industrialisation which transformed Russia's industries. He decided that modernising Russia meant:

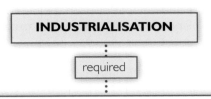

INDUSTRIALISATION

required

STATE ACTION

in order to provide the infrastructure (particularly railways) for a vast country of poor roads and few rivers running east–west. Under Witte's guidance the length of railways in Russia increased from 23,000 km in 1881 to 64,000 km by 1906. His greatest achievement was the 6000 km long Trans-Siberian railway.

For this ambitious programme, Witte needed **CAPITAL**

Russian capitalists were now encouraged (there were few of them in 'old' Russia).

Foreign investment was essential as there weren't enough capitalists in Russia ready to invest in industry. Nearly half of the capital invested in Russian industry came from abroad, much of it from France.

Capitalist
Someone who invests money in expectation of receiving a percentage in return, as a dividend

pig-iron
Ingots of iron, after smelting, ready to be used to make something

For more on **Sergei Witte** see page 32.

As a result of these developments, industrial production increased by 6 to 8 per cent every five years from 1885 onwards – the fastest growth rate in the world. Coal, iron and oil industries grew up in the Ukraine, Georgia and Azerbaijan. Huge textile and engineering works developed in Moscow, St Petersburg and the Baltic provinces. Production of coal multiplied eight times from 1880 to 1910, of **pig iron** multiplied seven times and of oil multiplied by eighteen times.

By 1900, Witte's industrialisation programme brought massive growth for the Russian economy but the human cost was terrible. Large factories were more profitable for foreign investors: many employed over 1000 workers. Wages were low. Hours were long. Accidents were common, and uncompensated – there were 500 fatalities in 1905 in the metallurgical industries alone. Foremen were allowed to beat workers. Young children were regularly employed. And as we've seen (page 14), workers resented the lack of respect shown by foremen addressing them as *tyi* (you), rather than the more formal *vyi*.

There were laws to prevent the worst abuses: child labour was regulated in 1882, schooling for factory children was to be provided and women's night work reduced. But these laws were widely ignored, and there were not nearly enough inspectors to enforce them.

Housing conditions were appalling: overcrowded, insanitary, lacking in all amenities and privacy. In St Petersburg there were on average sixteen people to an apartment, with six to a room. Curtains, or board partitions, divided up rooms for each family. Worse conditions existed in the lodging-houses, where whole families lived in dormitories, with only a bed to define their living-space.

St Petersburg had a population of nearly 1.5 million by 1900, and rising fast, with Moscow not far behind. Factories poured their refuse into rivers and canals, along with human waste. There was no safe water to drink and cholera epidemics returned in one year out of every three. Life expectancy in 1897 in St Petersburg was 37.

See also pages 13–14 for further discussion of industrial workers' problems.

△ Building the Trans-Siberian Railway. Notice the number of workers – 90,000 were needed for the whole 6000 km of the railway – and the amount of iron – vast amounts were needed for the whole track.

△ Living space for four Moscow workers, about 1900. Two-thirds of the population of St Petersburg had been born in a village and 90 per cent of workers sent money home to relatives in the countryside. Trotsky, with his typical flair for a phrase, described them as 'snatched from the plough and hurled straight into the factory furnace'.

Of course, the workers protested. In early days these protests looked like peasant violence transferred to the city. For example, an unpopular foreman would often be forced into a wheelbarrow and tipped into the canal. By the late 1890s, however, protests were changing: 97,000 workers took part in strikes in 1897. This suggests that workers were getting more organised.

Nicholas refused to do anything about the situation of the workers. He wanted Russia to be a modern industrial country, but turned a blind eye to what this meant for the workers. He was hostile to allowing the workers to set up trade unions, a concession which might have moderated worker demands, because he was opposed to all forms of organisation not under the control of his government.

recession
A decline in business and trade

The situation grew worse when a world-wide **recession** from 1900 meant that factories cut wages or laid workers off. There was no unemployment insurance in Russia. The streets of the cities became crowded with gangs of the unemployed. The army was called out to suppress workers' protests on 522 occasions in 1902. Unlike the situation in western Europe, it was the skilled, better-paid workers who were most militant, the most affected by the Marxist opposition parties you will read about on pages 43–44.

Factor 4

1 Why did industrial conditions lead to anger amongst workers?

2 How much was Nicholas to blame for the conditions experienced by workers at home and in factories? Now continue Activity 2b on page 31, annotating your causation map with a large 'N', a small 'N', or none at all, depending on your decision.

Anger amongst national and ethnic minorities

Russification

Alexander III began, Pobedonostsev guided and Nicholas continued the policy of Russification. This meant that the government was determined to promote Russians, the Russian language, Russian Orthodox religion and the Russian culture, over all others. Russian was the only official language, in education, the law-courts and government, even in areas where few people spoke it. Non-Russians made up 44 per cent of the population, but Russians were put in charge of non-Russian provinces, which were made to pay heavy taxes to the Russian government. Nicholas was a strong supporter of Russification and, as you have seen in all his policies, he preferred repression over concessions to the rights of the national and ethnic minorities who made up over half his subjects.

The reaction of national minorities to Russification is often under-played in textbooks which tend to follow only what went on in St Petersburg and Moscow. The late nineteenth and early twentieth century was a time of rising national feeling all over Europe, not only in politics but in music, culture, religion, language and literature. Russification swam against this tide. Poles, Finns, Lithuanians, Latvians, Estonians, as well as the peoples of the Caucasus and south east Russia had their own long-standing cultures, languages and their own leaders. There were religious differences: Poland was Roman Catholic, Lithuania was Lutheran, Georgia had its own, ancient, Orthodox Church and millions of Muslims lived under Russian rule. In all these cases local identity was discriminated against. Not surprisingly, national minorities and ethnic minorities, particularly Jews, were disproportionately represented among the opposition groups.

◁ This Muslim couple were photographed in Dagestan between 1905–15. Dagestan was a province in the far south of the Russian Empire, in the Caucasus Mountains to the west of the Caspian Sea (see the map on pages 2–3).

39

Anti-Semitism

▷ Banned from running schools, Jews sent their children to the rabbi to be instructed in their religion.

The Pale
Jews were not allowed to live in Russia itself. They were only permitted to live in parts of the Ukraine, Belorus, Poland and Lithuania which became known as the 'Pale'

Okhrana
The Tsar's police

Factor 6

1 Why was anger increasing among national and ethnic minorities in the years before 1905?

2 To what extent was Nicholas responsible for their resentment and anger? Now continue Activity 2b on page 31, annotating your causation map.

There were five million Jews in Russia in the late nineteenth century. They already suffered from discrimination, barred from living in much of Russia, forced to live in the '**Pale**'. From 1881 onwards they were to suffer from increasingly fierce anti-Semitism, encouraged and financed by government ministers, condoned by the Tsars and the Orthodox Church.

Following the assassination of Alexander II in 1881, Jewish-owned shops and houses were broken into and smashed up in the search for scapegoats. Jews were beaten, raped and killed. The word 'pogrom', a Russian word for destructive violence, was used to describe these attacks and has come to be used for all anti-Semitic violence. Over the next few years, under Alexander III and Nicholas II, Jews in Russia suffered increasing discrimination in law, as well as growing personal violence. They were barred from owning land, running their own schools or publishing books in Hebrew. They could not marry a Christian, become a town mayor, practise as a lawyer or sell alcohol. A strict quota was imposed on numbers of Jews allowed into universities. These legal restrictions were accompanied by pogroms almost every year.

'The Protocols of the Elders of Zion', a document which purported to be a Jewish plan to take over the world, widely used by anti-Semites in Nazi Germany and elsewhere up to the present-day, was written by the **Okhrana** (see page 25) in 1902. After Nicholas's death, a copy of this infamous document was found in his possessions. He held the anti-Semitic views common among his advisers: '… *nine-tenths of the trouble-makers are Jews*' he wrote in 1905.

Not surprisingly, millions of Russian Jews left Russia in these years, many settling in Britain, other European countries and the USA. Jews, also not surprisingly, played a disproportionate role in many opposition groups.

The growth of opposition groups

Next time you read about a ruler being driven out of power violently, see if you can discover which of these things were missing in that country:

- The right to organise alternative political parties.
- The right to meet, discuss and publish criticism of the government in the media.
- The right to change the government by democratic means.
- The right of peaceful street demonstration.

The chances are that none of them were present. And none were present in tsarist Russia, either. There was no parliament, so no point in forming parties. Organised opposition groups were illegal. The press was heavily censored. Underground newspapers circulated secretly, but their writers, printers, distributors and even their readers faced arrest and long prison sentences if caught. Street protests were violently broken up by police and soldiers, often the brutal, hated **Cossacks**, fiercely loyal to the Tsar. The *Okhrana* used paid informers to discover and arrest opponents. Revolutionaries had to run their organisations from abroad.

The only places where dissent could form, where people could meet, talk, question and share radical ideas, were the universities. Most of the tiny number of opposition members were radicalised at university. Entry to many of the usual career paths open to graduates – the law, medicine, teaching, publishing, finance, the civil service – was closed by corruption, discrimination against non-Russians and anti-Semitism.

Cossacks
Horsemen from the Ukraine, in the south of the Russian Empire. They were given special privileges in return for fighting for the Tsars

Opposition groupings in early twentieth century Russia

Marxist Revolutionaries				Reformists
Social Democrats		**Social Revolutionaries (SRs)**		**Liberals**
Industrial worker-based		Peasant-based		Middle class-based
Bolsheviks	Mensheviks	Left SRs	Right SRs	Kadets
Russia should go straight to a proletarian revolution. Tight-knit, centralised party to lead workers towards revolution.	Russia had to have a bourgeois revolution first. Open, democratic party. Supported the growth of trade unions.	All land should be taken from upper classes and shared out among the peasants. Tactics taken on from the 'People's Will': terrorism, assassinations (see page 43).	All land should be taken from upper classes and shared out among the peasants. Tactics – argument, persuasion.	More democracy, rule of law, free speech, free press, more education.

Liberal middle class reformists

▷ This photograph shows three generations of the Kalganov family, at the arms factory at Zlatoust, in the Ural Mountains. The father wears traditional dress, but his son and grand-daughter wear smart modern clothes. They hold responsible jobs in the factory, but there was no political role for them in Nicholas' Russia, they could not vote, join political parties or criticise the Tsar.

Old Imperial Russia had only a tiny middle class of small town shopkeepers, but Witte's economic expansion created many more merchants, bankers, and industrialists. They were wealthy and well-travelled, powerful people. Also growing was the professional middle class: doctors, lawyers, teachers, agricultural experts, statisticians. Both groups supported Russia's active cultural life: the ballet, opera and theatre. But they were aware of differences between tsarist Russia and other European nations. In most of western Europe the middle classes had taken over from the aristocracy as the driving force in society. Middle class Russians who chose to do so could get involved in local councils, the *zemstvos*, but the civil service and the Tsar's court itself were closed to them. They also found the corruption and inefficiency of Russia frustrating.

Many educated middle class Russians and some nobles wanted to move peacefully to a freer, more democratic society. They believed in what we call 'liberal' values: more democracy, free speech, equality before the law and other basic rights. Although they had support in the local councils, the *zemstvos*, they found it hard to have any effect on tsarism. However, they were by no means revolutionaries. They had a lot to lose if there was a major upheaval. They looked at the illiterate peasants and rough workers with horror. A few concessions from the Tsar, a bit more democracy, a few doors opened to them, and most would be prepared to stand by him.

However, under Alexander III and Nicholas II, liberal reformers could only meet in secret. They published illegal newspapers, but the stumbling block was always going to be the obvious resistance of the Tsar to any move towards democracy. In 1903 a Union of Liberation was formed to campaign for more freedoms but the Liberals made little effort to gain support from the peasants and workers.

Factor 7

1 Summarise the reasons why middle class Russians resented Tsarism.

2 To what extent was Nicholas responsible for this resentment? Now continue Activity 2b on page 31, annotating your causation map.

Revolutionaries

Both tsarists and opponents of tsarism were inclined to over-romanticise the peasants. To the Tsar, they were simple, faithful and loyal. Opponents talked glowingly of the *mir*, the loyal community of the village, where everyone was equal, in a kind of peasant socialism. Both were wildly untrue, but that did not stop groups of young students, called Populists, going out from their universities in 1874 to live with the peasants and talk to them about revolution. The peasants thought they were hopeless dreamers, often handed them over to the police and used their leaflets as toilet paper. Although there were only about 2000 of them, the failure of the Populists had a profound effect on Russian revolutionary movements.

The People's Will

In the light of the failure of Populism and continuing tsarist repression, some turned to terrorist violence. The People's Will set out to assassinate members of the ruling class. They may have hoped such deeds would provoke an uprising of the people, or drive the government to ever more repressive action until eventually the people would rise up. It was this tiny, secret group who assassinated Alexander II in 1881. The group then declined under harassment from the *Okhrana*, but its ideas lived on.

Marxism

The ideas of **Karl Marx** had a profound effect on Russian intellectual revolutionaries. They seemed to be an accurate analysis of history, and of the political and economic situation in many European countries. Marxist 'laws' suggested that the longed-for revolution was inevitable. But there was a problem: Russia did not have the large industrial working class, the proletariat who, Marx said, would lead the revolution. Instead it had millions of peasants. How would Marxism apply to Russia? Intellectuals argued about this into many a long Russian night, but two main views formed around two Marxist opposition parties – the Social Revolutionaries and the Social Democrats.

> It would be a good idea to remind yourself of who **Karl Marx** was and what his ideas were by looking back to pages 20–21.

The Social Revolutionaries (SRs)

The Social Revolutionary Party came together in 1901, led by Victor Chernov. They argued that, with peasants making up 80 per cent of the population, any revolution in Russia had to come from them. They therefore supported peasant demands that the nobles' land should be seized and shared out. The SRs argued that the peasants would lead the revolution, bypassing the capitalist stage to a kind of rural socialism. They were the largest opposition group, with several thousand members, divided about equally between peasants and workers (who were, after all, not far removed from the villages). It was a loose party, only brought together in 1901 under Chernov's leadership. There were terrorist elements on one wing, the heirs of the People's Will. These 'Left SRs', were responsible for about 2000 assassinations between 1900 and 1905, including government ministers and the Tsar's uncle. However, most SRs were 'Right SRs' and much more moderate.

The Social Democrats (SDs)

The All-Russian Social Democratic Workers Party was founded in 1898 by George Plekhanov. He had translated Karl Marx's writings into Russian and was convinced that Witte's economic reforms brought revolution nearer by creating the industrial working class Marx had described. The Social Democrats began setting up workers' organisations and illegal trade unions in Moscow and St Petersburg.

This approach was attacked by **Lenin**, the rising influence in the SDs, on his return from exile in Siberia in 1900. Lenin argued that Plekhanov's policy of trying to be a broad-based party, working for better conditions for workers, would never bring about revolution. What was needed, given the lack of revolutionary zeal among the workers, was a small party of dedicated revolutionaries. To get his ideas across, he started a party newspaper, *Iskra* (The Spark), and in 1902 wrote a famous pamphlet called *What is to be done?*

At the 1903 Social Democratic Party congress the SDs split. In a key vote Lenin claimed a majority and his group became known as Bolsheviks, from the Russian word for a majority. The remainder of the Party, named, of course, the Russian for minority, were called Mensheviks. For a while membership of the two factions was fluid, but they soon began to drift apart.

> **Lenin** plays a central part in the story of this book. For details on the man himself, see pages 84–85.

The Social Democratic split, 1903

> We take the straightforward Marxist view: Russia is not yet ready for the workers' revolution – it has not yet had its bourgeois revolution, and this could take a long time. We have an open, democratic party, open to all and ready to work with other parties and trade unions.

> Our leader, Lenin, says that Russia could skip the bourgeois revolution phase and move straight to the proletarian revolution. To achieve this, the workers will have to be led and it is our job to lead them towards revolution. This requires a committed, tight-knit party under central control. Such an organisation would also be able to prevent infiltration by the secret police.

Menshevik

Bolshevik

Factor 8

1. To what extent was the likelihood of revolution increased by:
   a) the frustrations of liberal reformers?
   b) the actions and plans of revolutionaries?
2. How much was Nicholas to blame for these developments? Now continue Activity 2b on page 31, annotating your causation map.

Why then? What were the immediate causes of the 1905 Revolution?

- **Bad harvests** in 1902 and 1903 caused real hunger among the peasants (Factor 3).
- **Depression in the world economy** from 1900 caused millions of workers to face unemployment, with no welfare support to turn to (Factor 5).
- **Minority nationalities**, particularly the Poles, stepped up their protests.
- A *Zemstvo* Congress met in November 1904 and its liberal middle class members called for a democratic constitution. Banned from holding political meetings, liberals held 'banquets', at which political speeches were made.

The Russo–Japanese War, 1904–05

This did not look like a good moment to go to war, but Nicholas and his advisers thought differently. Their aim was to seize Manchuria and Korea. Despite the huge size of its land-mass, Russia lacked an ice-free Pacific port. Manchuria would provide this, and open up a new area for imperial expansion. It would also, they hoped, distract the Russian people from their grievances and unite them behind the Tsar. There was a racial element too: they assumed the Japanese, as non-Europeans, would be easy to defeat.

They could not have been more wrong. Japan had carried out a major and highly successful modernisation programme in the late nineteenth century. Their better-equipped and far better-led army and navy inflicted heavy defeats on the Russians. In January 1905 the Russian fort at Port Arthur fell to the Japanese after a long siege. In February, Japanese troops seized Mukden, the chief city in Manchuria. In an incredible and futile journey the Russian navy travelled round the world from the Baltic to the Sea of Japan, pausing only to fire their guns at some British fishing boats in the North Sea, thinking they were Japanese warships. The journey took eight months and the Russian fleet was heavily defeated off Tsushima in two days in May 1905. All their battleships and half their cruisers were sunk; 4380 sailors died.

If the war was intended to lift the nation, these humiliating defeats had the opposite effect. In an autocracy, there is nowhere else to place the blame for humiliating defeat but on the autocrat. It was Nicholas' advisers who wanted to go to war, even though they had obviously not bothered to assess Japanese military strength – but he chose those advisors. His generals and admirals made bad decisions, but it was Nicholas who appointed and promoted them from the tiny aristocratic class. Tsarism was shown to be not only tyrannical, but incompetent. It turned protests into revolution. As the disasters continued, the Tsar's ability to deal with opposition was fatally weakened.

> The factors we have been looking at – Tsarism, the problems of peasants, workers, national minorities and the crushing of the opposition – had all been present for some time. So why did everything come together in 1905? What were the triggers?

> **Factor 9**
> 1 How did the war increase the possibility of revolution?
> 2 Was Nicholas to blame for defeat by Japan and the other immediate causes listed above? Now continue Activity 2b on page 31, annotating your causation map.

> Refer also to the large map on pages 2–3.

▷ **Map showing areas involved in Russo–Japanese War, 1904–05.**

Dateline of the 1905 Revolution

The 1905 Revolution happened because the grievances of many different groups of people all came to a head at once, triggered by a weakening of the Tsar's position. There were therefore several sequences of events going on at once.

It can be confusing, but don't panic! This dateline pins down the most important events. Events are colour-coded according to who is taking part.

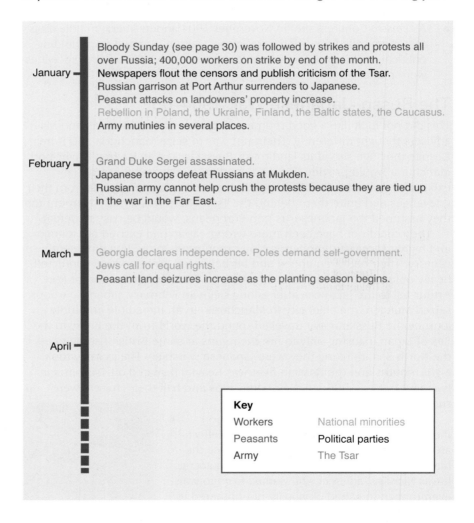

January
Bloody Sunday (see page 30) was followed by strikes and protests all over Russia; 400,000 workers on strike by end of the month.
Newspapers flout the censors and publish criticism of the Tsar.
Russian garrison at Port Arthur surrenders to Japanese.
Peasant attacks on landowners' property increase.
Rebellion in Poland, the Ukraine, Finland, the Baltic states, the Caucasus.
Army mutinies in several places.

February
Grand Duke Sergei assassinated.
Japanese troops defeat Russians at Mukden.
Russian army cannot help crush the protests because they are tied up in the war in the Far East.

March
Georgia declares independence. Poles demand self-government. Jews call for equal rights.
Peasant land seizures increase as the planting season begins.

April

Key

Workers	National minorities
Peasants	Political parties
Army	The Tsar

May

Liberal organisations combine in a Union of Unions. Its president, Paul Miliukov, demands *'the removal of the gang of robbers now in power and their replacement by a Constituent Assembly'*. Constitutional Democrat Party is formed (the KDs, or Kadets). Miliukov becomes the leader of the party.

Soviets (elected factory committees) begin to appear.

Russian naval fleet suffers catastrophic defeat at Tsushima.

June

Mutiny on battleship Potemkin. The sailors take the ship to Odessa where they join with striking workers. Troops disperse the sailors and crowds gathering on the steps leading to the waterfront. Thousands are shot and killed by government troops. The Potemkin mutineers sail to Romania, where they abandon the ship.

All over Russia, peasants drive landowners and their families out, set fire to their houses and buildings, seize and redistribute land.

July

All-Russian Peasants Union demands 'private property in land should be abolished … The land should be the common property of the whole people'.

August

Tsar Nicholas talks of an elected Assembly, but with only advisory powers and a franchise which would exclude most workers, all Jews and all women. This is rejected by the KaDets and ignored by everyone else.

Treaty of Portsmouth (USA) with Japan. The army are now free to return to help the Tsar regain control.

September

A strike by railway workers paralyses the country. The government are unable to get troops around the country to suppress protests.

General strikes: two million workers involved. Some employers support the strike.

October

St Petersburg workers set up a soviet as an alternative government, acting in co-ordination with other city soviets. Leon Trotsky, a brilliant organiser and speaker (and a Menshevik at this time) elected Chairman. One third of the army is weakened by mutinies.

General strikes all over Russia. No telephones, no water supply, no street lights.

Nicholas recalls Witte, who recommends making concessions. Nicholas is reluctant, until his uncle, Grand Duke Nicholas, threatens to shoot himself if he doesn't.

Nicholas issues the October Manifesto which conceeds:
• an elected parliament (or *duma*), with a wide franchise
• full civil liberties, including free speech, religious toleration and freedom to organise protests.

Trotsky played a central role in later events. For more information about him, see pages 114–115.

It seemed like it was the end of tsarist autocracy.

For a few months culminating in the early autumn of 1905 all the forces ranged against the Tsar came together while his own position was low:

THE TSAR'S OPPONENTS

Liberals who provided leadership, and a platform: the demand for a democratic assembly – a *duma*.

+

Workers whose strikes brought industry to a standstill.

+

Students whose demonstrations took over the streets.

+

Peasants who were attacking landowners' property.

+

National minorities who held mass demonstrations in many cities.

THE 1905 CONTEXT

Tsarist government whose reputation was lowered and whose incompetence was revealed by defeat in the **Russo-Japanese war**.

+

Army which was busy in the Far East, so unable to support the government.

+

Violence: over 1000 assassinations took place between February 1905 and May 1906, a quarter of whom were senior government officials.

+

World economic **depression**

■ But is it going to last?

Use this page to think about whether the unity of the Tsar's opponents would hold together after the publication of the Tsar's October Manifesto and how long the 1905 context would last.

■ Concluding your Enquiry

Look at the causation map you've built up throughout this enquiry.

1 Your causation map shows how much you think Nicholas was to blame for the 1905 Revolution, with a large letter 'N' next to a factor meaning he was completely or mostly to blame, a small 'N' meaning he was partly to blame, and no letter meaning he was not to blame at all.

Do your annotations already suggest that Nicholas was mainly responsible?

2 Now the next stage:

a) What links can you draw between the different individual factors? Draw lines across the diagram, linking factors which supported each other.

b) Review your diagram using the information in the dateline of the 1905 Revolution (pages 46–47) and the chart opposite, to add to or make changes to the links you've drawn. (You might, for example, want to look at how big a part opposition parties played in the events of 1905.)

3 Do the links support the view that Nicholas was MAINLY responsible for the Revolution? If there are several factors that don't link to him at all then he can't have been MAINLY responsible.

And what do I think?

Don't ignore the 'trigger' causes even though we have given more space to the longer-term factors. The Revolution took place in 1905, not 1904, or 1900 or 1895. The historian Beryl Williams suggests that it was the world-wide depression which plunged the already difficult lives of the workers into unemployment and desperation. It was then the overwhelming and humiliating defeat of the army and navy in the war with Japan which destroyed any lingering respect the people may have had for tsarism.

However the Revolution did grow out of tsarism and Nicholas' own failure. The main causes of unrest and dissatisfaction with tsarism amongst liberals, workers, peasants and national minorities are obvious and have been given plenty of space in this enquiry. British historian Orlando Figes is very clear where he puts the blame: *'Nicholas was the source of all the problems. If there was a vacuum at the centre of the ruling system, then he was the empty space.'*

He certainly inherited a system of government that belonged to another era. By choosing to industrialise Russia without democratising it, his predecessors had set a course that created the tensions which broke out in revolution. However, by doing nothing, Nicholas made things worse. He was too small-minded and bound in to his upbringing and education to change Russia's system of government.

I would go further than Figes: in several ways he actively made things worse. For his Russification and anti-Semitism, his readiness to use force to crush his people, and his callous disregard for their sufferings, he is to blame. I cannot accept the sentimental view that he was a good little man lost in a situation too big for him. As you will see in the next enquiry, such a view ignores too much.

4 Russia in 1914: On the verge of revolution? Or becoming a Western-style democracy?

△ Huge cheering crowds greet the Tsar as he rides into Moscow for the tercentenary celebrations of the Romanov dynasty, 1913.
Is this picture evidence that Nicholas was now popular?

The celebrations in 1913 of 300 years of the Romanov dynasty gave the tsarist government opportunities for spectacular pageantry. It started with Nicholas and his family proceeding by open horse-drawn carriages to a solemn service in the Kazan Cathedral in St Petersburg. A national holiday had been declared and free meals were served in the poorer parts of the city. There was a public fireworks display in the evening, followed by a week of receptions and balls at the Winter Palace. In the summer the royal party went on a tour of the old heartlands of Russia by royal train and a convoy of 20 motor cars. The last event was the entry into Moscow, with Nicholas riding a white horse, alone, 20 metres in front of his guards.

These events were the first occasions Nicholas had ridden in public since the 1905 Revolution. Do the sheer numbers of people on the Moscow streets in this picture suggest that the bitterness towards him had been forgotten? If so, Russia was no longer on the verge of revolution. A year later, on 30 July 1914, Tsar Nicholas ordered the mobilisation of his vast army, and so took Russia into the First World War. This enquiry investigates what Russia was like as it entered the war. Was it still a backward autocracy that was threatened by revolution or was Russia turning into a modern industrialised democracy, free from fear of revolution?

■ **Enquiry Focus:** Russia in 1914: on the verge of revolution, or becoming a Western-style democracy?

This enquiry is an <u>interpretation</u> question, investigating historians' interpretations of conditions in Russia in 1914. Some historians of the Russian Revolution are known as 'Optimists' because they argue that things were getting better by 1914, that Russia was well on the way to becoming a western-style democracy and seemed to have staved off the threat of violent revolution. Other historians, however, argue that Russia had not changed in its essentials and that revolution was still highly likely.

Why is this debate on the condition of Russia in 1914 important? It's important because it helps us understand the differing explanations of why the Revolution broke out in 1917. The <u>Optimists' hypothesis</u>, that Russia was well on the way to becoming a modern democracy, suggest that the 1917 Revolution was not inevitable but the result of the unpredictable circumstances of the First World War.

The Optimists develop their case by pointing out that in Russia in 1914:

1 **The forces of violent revolution had been stifled**. The 1905 October Manifesto gave the liberals what they had called for: a constitution, free speech, religious toleration, freedom to organise. It separated them off from the radicals and revolutionaries. The government then set about crushing revolutionary opposition groups with a tough and well-organised programme of repression.

2 **Russia was becoming a functioning democracy.** There was a parliament (the *duma*) with elections, parties and real debates, so there was no need for a revolution.

3 **Russia had a boom economy with a middle class increasing in size and importance**. The Russian economy was booming, led by the armaments industry. This boom particularly benefitted the middle classes, which grew in both numbers and wealth. They were much more likely to be supporters of moderation than revolution.

4 **Many of the peasants' grievances had been dealt with**. Nicholas' able minister, Piotr Stolypin, had carried out major reforms giving peasants a real opportunity to break out of poverty. Russia was well on the way to having a class of successful peasant farmers with a vested interest in supporting the tsarist system.

5 **Many workers were better off**. Booming industry brought better wages, especially for skilled workers, who would, it was hoped, become less revolutionary. In time, all workers would share in this prosperity and abandon their revolutionary attitudes.

The pages which follow deal with each point on the list, one by one. As you read them, judge whether the Optimists are right about each of the five points. The Optimists' hypothesis is unlikely to be 100 per cent right or 100 per cent wrong; you will have to make a judgement about **how far** each of the Optimists' cases has been proved and mark its position on the Revolution/Democracy line below.

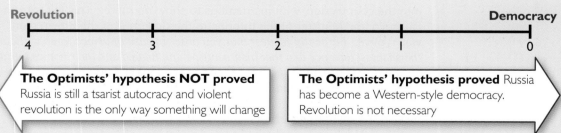

Revolution   **Democracy**

4   3   2   I   0

The Optimists' hypothesis NOT proved
Russia is still a tsarist autocracy and violent revolution is the only way something will change

The Optimists' hypothesis proved Russia has become a Western-style democracy. Revolution is not necessary

The Optimists' case: 1. The forces of violent revolution had been stifled

First we need to return to 1905. Nicholas' 'October Manifesto' (see pages 47 and 54) was welcomed on the streets. There were cheering crowds, speakers on the corners testing the new freedom of speech, the general strike was called off, in Poland, Lithuania, Finland and other non-Russian-speaking parts of the Empire, newspapers appeared in the local languages. However, despite this optimism, the tsarist government was about to regain control of the country.

To the revolutionaries the promise of an elected *duma* did not go nearly far enough, but the public were pleased by the promise of an elected *duma* and so the revolutionaries lost support and were isolated.

This was exactly what Witte had calculated when he persuaded Nicholas to grant the October Manifesto.

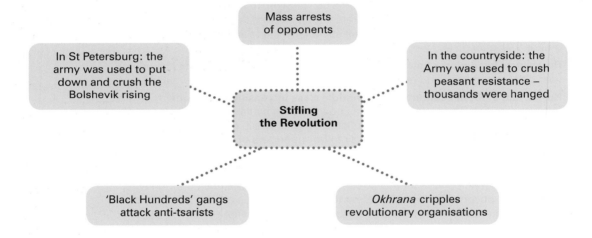

Mass arrests of opponents

In St Petersburg: the army was used to put down and crush the Bolshevik rising

In the countryside: the Army was used to crush peasant resistance – thousands were hanged

Stifling the Revolution

'Black Hundreds' gangs attack anti-tsarists

Okhrana cripples revolutionary organisations

Soviet
A council elected by factory workers

By December 1905 the government decided to move against the revolutionaries. Troops loyal to the Tsar arrested most of the members of the St Petersburg **Soviet**. An armed rising in Moscow instigated by the Bolsheviks was brutally put down: working class districts were shelled, hundreds were arrested and executed. At least 1000 people died.

Meanwhile there was also tough repression in the countryside. Peasants could not see anything for them in the October Manifesto and continued their attacks on property into November. The government sent troops out into the countryside, with instructions to show no mercy. This letter from Durnovo, the Minister of the Interior, to the Governor of the Kiev region was typical: *'I urgently request that you order the use of armed force without the slightest leniency and that insurgents be annihilated and their homes burnt.'*

Military courts held rapid trials and executions. 15,000 peasants were hanged, 45,000 deported. As Stolypin, Nicholas' Chief Minister from 1906, said: *'The punishment of a few prevents a sea of blood.'* Nicholas approved: he said the military governors were *'acting splendidly'*.

In addition, the government sponsored an organisation called The Union of Russian People. Like the Nazi brownshirts a few years later, it attracted working class right wing men who enjoyed a fight. Nicknamed the 'Black Hundreds', their victims were liberals, socialists and, especially, Jews. Gangs carried icons and pictures of the Tsar as well as knives and knuckle-dusters. Anyone who seemed reluctant to kiss the icon or sing the national anthem was beaten up. Over 3000 people were killed by the Black Hundreds in 1905–06. Nicholas wore their badge (he blamed 'the Jews' for the revolution anyway) and the government provided money for their newspapers, transport and weapons.

One of the few government organisations which was really effective in the years up to 1917 was the secret police, the *Okhrana*. They operated virtually outside the law, with techniques other secret security forces have used since: spying on revolutionary organisations, opening mail, tapping telephones, bugging rooms, card indexing suspects. They were highly successful at 'turning' members of revolutionary organisations. A mixture of torture, beatings, cups of tea and offers of money led many former revolutionaries to spy on their colleagues. From the information received, the *Okhrana* made sudden mass arrests of key members, usually in the middle of the night. Both the **SR** and the Bolsheviks were crippled by these *Okhrana* activities even at the highest levels. By 1917 most Bolshevik leaders had been living in exile abroad for many years and the SR organisation had collapsed.

How did Nicholas get away with it? Through 1906, parts of Russia were close to a state of civil war. Militant revolutionaries fought back: it is estimated that about 2000 government officials were killed. But the government was bound to win in the end because:

△ This cartoon shows Tsar Nicholas and his daughters. It was published in a German magazine critical of tsarism. The sarcastic caption was: 'The Prince of Peace. Now I have peace with my people.'

Here again is Point 1 of the Optimist historians' case

1 The forces of violent revolution had been stifled.

1 Whereabouts on the Revolution/Democracy line would you put the government's actions towards the revolutionaries? How far does the evidence prove that the Optimists' Point 1 is true?

2 Explain in your own words why you have put it in that position.

- Its opponents were disunited. Workers, peasants, middle class liberals, nationalists, moderates and revolutionaries had little in common with each other apart from anger with the Tsar. There was no leader to bring them together. It was relatively easy for skilled ministers like Witte and Stolypin to prise the groups apart.
- The army stayed loyal to Nicholas. There were mutinies, but they were restricted to local affairs and petered out when the war with Japan ended. In April 1906 Witte arranged a huge loan from the French government. This restored economic support for tsarism. It also enabled Nicholas to pay his troops to carry out their savage repression of his people.

SRs
Social Revolutionaries. Peasant based Socialist party (see page 43)

The Optimists' case: 2. Russia was becoming a functioning democracy

In the October Manifesto, Tsar Nicholas II had reluctantly broken 300 years of tradition and agreed to hold an elected duma. But was he ready to become a constitutional monarch? As you read this account of the opening ceremony of the First Duma in April 1906, in the Coronation Hall of the Tsar's Winter Palace, what clues does the historian Orlando Figes give us about Nicholas' attitude?

The throne was draped in ermine with the crown, the sceptre, the seal and the orb placed at its feet on four little stools. The miraculous icon of Christ was placed, like a holy protector, before it, and solemnly guarded by a retinue of high priests. The deep basses of the choir, dressed in cassocks of crimson and gold, sang verse after verse of 'God Save the Tsar', as if on purpose to keep the congregation standing, until, at the height of the fanfare's crescendo, the royal procession arrived.

On one side of the hall stood the great and good of autocratic Russia: state councillors, senators, ministers, admirals, generals and members of the court, all of them turned out in their brilliant dress uniforms dripping with medals and gold braid. Facing them were the parliamentary leaders of the new democratic Russia, a motley collection of peasants in cotton shirts and tunics, professional men in lounge suits, monks and priests in black, Ukrainians, Poles, Tartars

▽ The opening of the First Duma in April 1906.

and others in colourful national costumes, and a small number of nobles in evening dress.

'The two hostile sides stood confronting one another' recalled one who was there. 'The old and grey court dignitaries, keepers of etiquette and tradition, looked across in a haughty manner, though not without fear and confusion, at "the people off the street", whom the revolution had swept into the palace. One of the socialist deputies, a tall man in a worker's blouse, scrutinised the throne and the courtiers around it with obvious disgust. As the Tsar and his entourage entered the hall, he lurched forward and stared at them with an expression of hatred. For a moment it was feared that he might throw a bomb.

'The court side of the hall resounded with orchestrated cheers as the Tsar approached the throne. But the Duma deputies remained completely silent … The Tsar delivered a short and perfunctory speech…and got up to leave. The parliamentary era had begun … As the royal procession filed out of the hall, tears could be seen on the face of the Tsar's mother, the Dowager Empress. It had been "a terrible ceremony", she later confided to the Minister of Finance. For several days she was unable to calm herself from the shock of seeing so many commoners in the palace. "They looked at us as upon their enemies and I could not stop myself from looking at certain faces, so much did they seem to reflect a strange hatred for us all."'

(Orlando Figes, *A People's Tragedy*, London, 1996)

> ▓ Does this description support the Optimists' case that Russia was becoming a functioning democracy?

So began Russia's eleven year democratic experiment: it doesn't sound as if it's going to go well, does it?

A week before the First Duma met, Nicholas published what he called – ominously – the Fundamental Laws. It was a long way from the democratic constitutional monarchy which most Russians thought had been conceded in October.

- The State Council would become an upper house of the *duma*. Half its members would be appointed by the Tsar, half elected by tsarist bodies such as the Church, the nobles, the *zemstvos* and the universities.
- Any laws had to be agreed by the duma, the State Council and the Tsar. This effectively gave him a veto over anything the duma wanted to do.
- The Tsar could dissolve the duma at any time and issue laws by decree when it was not sitting.
- The Tsar appointed his own ministers, who were not in the *duma* and not answerable to it.
- The Tsar kept control of foreign policy, the armed forces and the administration.

It was clear that he thought of the duma as, at best, there to give him advice.

Voting rights were complicated. All men over 45 could vote, but only nobles elected their representatives directly to the duma. The rest of voters elected representatives to a 'college', which in turn elected duma members. The effect of this was that the vote from 1 noble was equivalent to 2 townsmen's votes, 15 peasant votes and 45 urban worker votes.

Four dumas were elected between 1906 and 1917. Even though Nicholas resented what he regarded as their 'interference' in government, he needed to impress potential friends and allies amongst foreign countries that Russia ws becoming more democratic. Voting systems were reformed twice to ensure more right-wing, less revolutionary members were elected, suggesting that Russia was still a long way from being a proper democracy. Even so, the dumas continued to try to influence the Tsar's government.

First Duma, April–July 1906

Despite all these restrictions, millions turned out to vote, although the Social Revolutionaries and Social Democrats regarded the duma as just a sop to the bourgeoisie and boycotted the elections. After the votes had been counted, the biggest party in the *duma* was the Constitutional Democrats, the KD or Kadets (see diagram on page 41 for where this party stood). The Tsar, believing that all the peasants were his loyal supporters, was shocked to find that the next biggest group was the **Trudoviks**, a peasant grouping which was more radical in its demands than the Kadets. Riding the wave of democratic fervour, the Kadets called for a truly democratic constitution, based on universal suffrage, the removal of the state council and with ministers responsible to the duma and, from the Trudoviks, compulsory takeover of all private land and its re-distribution to the peasants.

But the Kadets had miscalculated. It was no longer October 1905 and the Tsar was back in control. During the night of 8/9 July 1906 the duma was dissolved. Furious, the Kadets went to Finland (a Russian province at this time), and issued the Vyborg Manifesto, calling on the people to refuse to pay taxes or join the army. 'The people' took little notice and most of the deputies who went to Vyborg were arrested and imprisoned.

Trudoviks
A small, radical group of agrarian socialists who broke away from the SRs (Social Revolutionaries)

Second Duma, February–June 1907

The Second Duma proved just as radical as the first. Many Kadet leaders were in prison, but this time Social Revolutionaries and Mensheviks took part, winning 37 and 47 seats respectively. Speakers denounced the land reforms which Stolypin was introducing and again called for the nationalisation of land. At 6 a.m. on Sunday 3 June, the Second Duma was dissolved by the Tsar.

Third Duma, 1907–12

▽ The numbers of voters of different classes required to elect each deputy after the 1907 changes to the franchise.

At Stolypin's suggestion, the government changed the electoral system to ensure a more compliant duma. Massive weighting was given to landowner voters, while peasants, workers and national minorities lost out. It has been calculated that one per cent of the electorate now elected 300 of the 442 deputies. The table below puts it another way:

I Deputy was elected by:	Landowners	Wealthy businessmen	Lower middle class	Peasants	Workers
	230	1,000	15,000	60,000	125,000

Stolypin and the Tsar got what they wanted: the duma was now much more in the hands of the centre right and right wing. The biggest party was the Octobrists (moderate conservatives), so called because they accepted that the October Manifesto was as far along the road to reform as they wanted to go. There were also many right-wing deputies who resisted all change. However, duma members still questioned ministers and criticised many of Stolypin's proposals. The duma also passed legislation to set up schools for poor children and an insurance scheme for workers, providing unemployment pay and funding medical fees.

Fourth Duma, 1912–17

Stolypin was assassinated in 1911 and the ministers Nicholas appointed as his successors did not conceal their contempt for the duma. This annoyed even this right-wing duma, who openly criticised the government. In 1913 they passed a resolution warning the Tsar:

> The Minister of the Interior systematically scorns public opinion and ignores the wishes of the new duma … The Ministry's activities arouse dissatisfaction among the broad masses who have hitherto been peaceful. Such a situation threatens Russia with untold dangers.

Summary

The duma was a constitutional experiment which had already lost the support of most Russians. To be fair, everyone involved had little experience of democratic procedures. Speakers would not stay in their places, but walked about, adding comments to their friends as they passed. Arguments broke out. Ministers were not members of the duma. When they did appear in the chamber, they lectured the members. The duma (even the Third and Fourth Dumas) made little effort to build a co-operative relationship with ministers. And the Tsar hated it.

Here again is Point 2 of the Optimist historians' case

2 Russia was becoming a functioning democracy.

1 Whereabouts on the Revolution/Democracy line would you put the *duma*? How far does the evidence prove that the Optimists' Point 2 is true?

2 Explain in your own words why you have put it in that position.

A cartoon from an opposition newspaper in 1906 called 'Voting in the Duma'. What can you infer from this cartoon about the cartoonist's views on: (i) free speech (ii) pressure from upper class deputies on others?

The Optimists' case: 3. Russia had a boom economy with a middle class increasing in size and importance

One of the triggers for the discontent which provoked the 1905 Revolution was a world recession (see page 45). This played itself out by about 1908 and the last few years of the tsarist economy were startlingly successful.

Factory at Kyn, east ▷ central Russia, 1912, photographed by Prokhudin-Gorskii.

	1910	1913
Pig iron production	3.00	5.00
Coal production	16.00	36.00
Consumption of cotton goods	0.36	0.43

△ Table A: production and consumption, in millions of tonnes.

	1910	1913
Value of imports	1.084	(not known)
Value of exports	1.448	1.520

△ Table B: Financial trade balance, in millions of roubles.

	1910	1913
Ordinary budget revenue from taxes	2.781	3.417
Ordinary budget expenditure	2.473	3.094

△ Table C: Government revenue balance, in millions of roubles.

Do statistics bring you out in a cold sweat? They can sometimes tell you a lot more than words. Let's take the three tables opposite.

Table A

Pig iron and coal are the essentials of heavy industry, and you can see that production of both more or less doubled. This was driven by a major rearmament programme, starting in 1912. But you can't eat or wear pig iron or coal: what about the ordinary Russian going shopping? The last row gives us a clue: a substantial increase in the amount of cotton goods produced, for example shirts, dresses, bed linen and so on. This suggests that ordinary Russians had money to spend. It also suggests that a demand for consumer goods would create more jobs.

The last two tables show the success of the Russian government economy.

Tables B and C

A healthy economy sells more than it buys (that is, its exports are worth more than its imports – Table B).

A healthy government budget spends less than it collects (Table C).

This growing modern economy created lots of middle class jobs, not only industrialists and bankers, but middle managers and clerks, as well as professionals such as lawyers, teachers and engineers. But were these new middle class Russians happy supporters of tsarism?

The 1905 Revolution left the Russian middle classes in a dilemma. Although they were increasing in numbers, importance and wealth, they were not increasing their influence. They were the main supporters of the Kadets and the Octobrists who, as we have seen, were getting sidelined in the duma. The Tsar's government, and the Third and Fourth Dumas, were in the hands of the old landowning classes. Middle class Russians looked enviously at western European countries, where the middle classes were dominant. They grumbled at the continuing incompetence and corruption of tsarism.

But what could they do about it? The last thing they wanted was a revolution. They had too much to lose and were not going to throw in their lot with the angry, revolutionary working class. In a remark which has become famous, the Kadet (and ex-Marxist) Peter Struve exclaimed as the 1905 revolution ended: *'Thank God for the Tsar who has saved us from the people'.*

Here again is Point 3 of the Optimist historians' case

> 3 Russia had a boom economy with a middle class increasing in size and importance.

Also bear in mind what you've just found out about the workings of the *duma*. Was the increase in the numbers and wealth of the middle classes moving Russia away from autocracy, towards democracy, as the Optimists claim, or not?

1 Whereabouts on the Revolution/Democracy line would you put economic developments? How far does the evidence prove that the Optimists' Point 3 is true?

2 Explain in your own words why you have put it in that position.

The Optimists' case: 4. Many of the peasants' grievances had been dealt with

A newspaper reported the peasant violence in 1905:

> Hundreds of buildings worth several million roubles have been destroyed. All the buildings have been razed to the ground on some large estates. Many houses have been burnt down, regardless of the relations between the peasants and the landowner. The farms of some well-known *zemstvo* liberals have been burnt along with the rest.

SRs were the Social Revolutionaries, a popular peasant-based revolutionary party. The Trudoviks had broken away from the SRs. Look back to page 41 to see more about SR beliefs and demands.

At the root of peasants' grievances was land hunger. In western Russia, for example, 100,000 landowners farmed one-third of the land, usually the best land, while twelve million peasants tried to make a living from the rest. The population of Russia rose by 21 per cent from 1900 to 1910, producing even more pressure on land as the *mir* tried to ensure that every household was given enough to live on. Furthermore, most peasants were carrying huge debts from emancipation. These, and the strength of the tradition for the farming methods the *mir* favoured, held back innovation and productivity was low. For most peasants the solution seemed clear: they should take over the land in the hands of private landowners because they were the ones who had worked it for generations. This was the demand of the **SRs** and the peasant Trudoviks in the duma.

Stolypin's policies

Nicholas was lucky to have in his service from 1906 an extremely able minister, Piotr Stolypin. He had not made his way to the top among the officials at St Petersburg but as a provincial governor of Saratov. There he had seen both the problems of the peasants and their revolutionary violence. He had used force to deal with peasant uprisings in his province and then organised the ferocious nationwide repression of 1906 (described on page 52), leading to the hangman's noose being nicknamed 'Stolypin's necktie'.

He set about a programme of land reform:

- Peasants were allowed to leave the *mir*.
- Those who left were encouraged to consolidate their scattered strips of land into a single farm.
- The Peasant Land Bank lent money to peasants to invest in new farming methods.
- In 1907 debts from redemption payments dating back to 1861 were cancelled.
- Six million hectares of state land in Siberia was made available to new settlers.

Octobrists
Moderate liberals who supported the Tsar's 1905 October Manifesto and believed that it was as far down the road towards democracy as Russia should go

Stolypin was a firm supporter of tsarism. He intended his programme to take the wind out of the sails of the peasant radicals in the SRs and Trudoviks and was supported in the duma by the **Octobrists**. He believed that peasants were naturally conservative and changes were needed to create a new class of successful, independent smallholding farmers, with a stake in the tsarist system. They would have the enterprise to improve their farming methods and increase yields, providing food for the cities and for export. Those with too little land would sell it and become wage labourers. The communal power of the *mir* would be broken and a capitalist economy take over the countryside. He called it *'A wager, not on the drunken and feeble, but on the sober and strong'*.

Stolypin said it would take twenty years to make the changes he wanted. He only had five: he was assassinated by Dmitiri Bogov, a member of the Social Revolutionary Party, at the Kiev Opera House in 1911. By then his reforms were making him unpopular among the big landowners who dominated the Tsar's court and his successors made less effort to continue with them, as the chart below suggests.

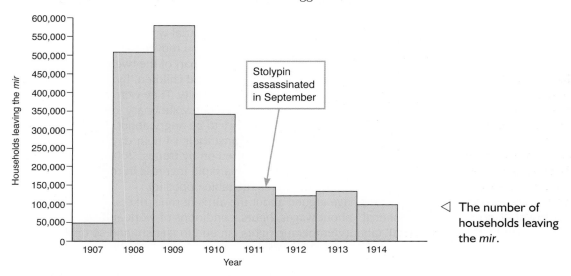

◁ The number of households leaving the *mir*.

How successful was Stolypin's 'wager on the strong'?

■ Peasants owned more land. Both the nobles and the state had been getting out of farming for many years and sold their land to the peasants. In 1877 peasants owned less than one-third of the land; by 1917 it was nearly half.

■ By 1914 two million peasants had left the *mir* (although this was only 10 per cent of all peasants, and by no means all of those who left the *mir* consolidated their strips into single smallholdings).

■ By 1913 three million settlers had taken up land in Siberia (although about half a million returned).

■ Agricultural productivity increased (although this was on both *mir* and independent peasant farms).

■ The countryside was relatively quiet between 1909 and 1913 (although this was probably due to good harvests as much as Stolypin's reforms).

Here again is Point 4 of the Optimist historians' case

4 Many of the peasants' grievances had been dealt with.

1 Whereabouts on the Revolution/Democracy line would you put the situation of the peasants? How far does the evidence prove that the Optimists' Point 4 is true?

2 Explain in your own words why you have put it in that position.

The Optimists' case: 5. Many workers were better off

Stolypin largely ignored the industrial workers. Subdued after the 1905 Revolution, their grievances nevertheless remained: low wages (they earned less than one-third of western European workers), long hours, dangerous working conditions, dreadful housing. From 1912, some workers were covered by an insurance scheme against accidents and illness, but for most there was no welfare system to deal with desperate poverty brought about by old age, unemployment or injury at work.

There was another important change taking place. As you saw on page 13, in the nineteenth century most of the industrial workers in Russian cities had been peasants from the countryside who moved to the city (sometimes only temporarily) to find work. By the first part of the twentieth century more workers had settled in the city and had children. By 1914 the majority of industrial workers had been born in the city. They were more literate than most peasants, ready to read and listen to revolutionary ideas.

The government gave them plenty to be angry about. In 1912 workers in the Lena goldfields, on strike against their 14-hour day, low pay and terrible working conditions, were fired on by troops. 200 were killed and many injured. This was followed by a rapid increase in the number of workers involved in strikes (see the table opposite).

Historians have argued about the aims of the strikers. Were they 'non-political' (about wages, hours, conditions of work and so on) or 'political' (about democratic rights, an end to tsarism and so on)? The classification in the table opposite was made by the police, so historians

▽ Strikers outside the Putilov steel and armaments works in 1905. This was one of the largest factories in Europe with 13,000 workers by 1913.

have to be cautious about the evidence. However, Soviet historians got excited about the apparent rise in the number of 'political' strikes from 1912 which you can see in the table. below. They say this proves that the workers were beginning to take the lead in the move towards the great proletarian revolution. They claim that this growing politicisation of the workers was due to the increasing influence of the Bolsheviks, especially in the large factories, such as the Putilov Works in St Petersburg. However, R B McKean's research in the 1980s showed that more workers were employed in small-scale, domestic and service employment than in heavy industry. He also found that, until 1917, far more days were lost in 'non-political' strikes than 'political' strikes.

	Number of workers involved in strikes	Number of strikes	Number of strikes classified as 'political'
1911	105,110	466	24
1912	725,491	2,032	1,300
1913	861,289	2,404	1,034
1914 (Jan–July)	1,448,684	3,534	2,401

△ Details of strikes between 1911 and 1914.

Here again is Point 5 of the Optimist historians' case

5 Many workers were better off.

1 Whereabouts on the Revolution/Democracy line would you put the government's actions towards the revolutionaries? How far does the evidence prove that the Optimists' Point 5 is true?
2 Explain in your own words why you have put it in that position.

■ Concluding your enquiry

1 Look back over where you have placed the five cases made by the Optimist historians on the Revolution/Democracy continuity line.

Discuss your decisions with others. It is often helpful to do this as others may have thought of something you missed. Even if they haven't, you'll find yourself having to defend your point of view, which helps clarify your thoughts.

2 What is your 'Headline answer'? For example:

'Russia was well on the way to becoming a democracy ...'

'While progress had been made, Russia was ...'

'Democracy stood no chance of developing while Nicholas was Tsar ...'

Use these headlines, or one of your own, to write an extended paragraph summarising your answer.

3 The historian (and former US Cold War presidential adviser) George Kennan writes here about how his views have changed.

a) What had Kennan originally believed about the situation in Russia before 1914?

b) How had he changed his views of this Optimists' interpretation?

c) Use your work on the activities in this enquiry to comment on the strengths and weaknesses of Kennan's change of mind.

I was inclined to feel that, had the [First World] war not intervened, the chances for survival of the autocracy and for its gradual evolution into a constitutional monarchy would not have been bad. On reviewing once more the events of these last decades, I find myself obliged to question that opinion. Neither the tardiness in the granting of political reform, nor the excesses of an extravagant and foolish nationalism, nor the personal limitations of the imperial couple began with the war or were primarily responses to the existence of the war. None of the consequences of these deficiencies were in the process of any significant correction as the war approached.

(George Kennan, quoted by Christopher Read in *In Search of Liberal Tsarism*, 1969)

How Russia entered the First World War

The story of how the governments of the Great Powers of Europe got themselves into a horrendous war which killed ten million of their citizens doesn't show any of them up in a good light; Nicholas' decisions were no more misguided and misinformed than those of several other rulers.

What drove Nicholas to take the decisions he did in 1914?

One of the driving forces of his reign was the promotion of everything Russian. The Russians defined themselves ethnically as a Slav people (as opposed to Germans and Austrians) and religiously as Christian Orthodox (as opposed to Roman Catholic or Protestant Christians). Outside Russia

this meant giving support to Serbia (a nation of Christian Orthodox Slavs) against Austro-Hungarian aggression in the Balkans (south-east Europe – see the map below). Austria–Hungary's ambitions in that area were also worrying for Russia because 40 per cent of its foreign trade passed through the Bosphorus and Dardanelles. Free passage through these narrow waterways was therefore vital and Austro-Hungarian control of them could exert a stranglehold on Russia. Further, Nicholas and his advisers were determined to re-establish Russia's honour and reputation after their humiliating defeat at the hands of the Japanese in 1905. This meant taking an aggressive line in diplomacy which was to prove fatal.

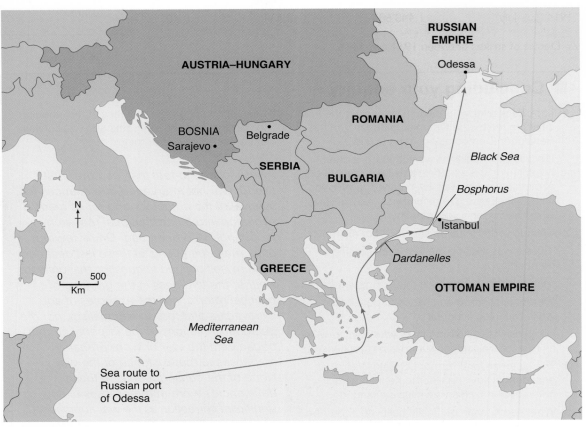

△ Eastern Europe and the Balkans in 1914.

The Austrian Archduke Franz Ferdinand was shot in Sarajevo on 28 June 1914, by Gavrilo Princip, a Serb. Austria-Hungary made threats against Serbia. At this point Nicholas had a series of telegram exchanges with his cousin, Wilhelm II, Kaiser of Germany, about how to avoid the crisis drifting into war. These 'Willy-Nicky' messages (in English) were friendly and Nicholas was sure war was unlikely. However, Austria-Hungary had obtained full German support for their aggressive moves and declared war on Serbia on 28 July. Nicholas ordered the mobilisation of the huge Russian army, expecting that this would scare Austria-Hungary off. Germany, however, had a war plan – the Schlieffen Plan. German generals' greatest fear was having to split their forces in a two-front war against both Russia and her ally, France. The Plan relied on Russia being slow to mobilise, giving just time for German forces to smash France. Their armies would then be transported by rail to deal with Russia. They could not afford to let Russia get ahead with their mobilisation, so declared war on 1 August 1914.

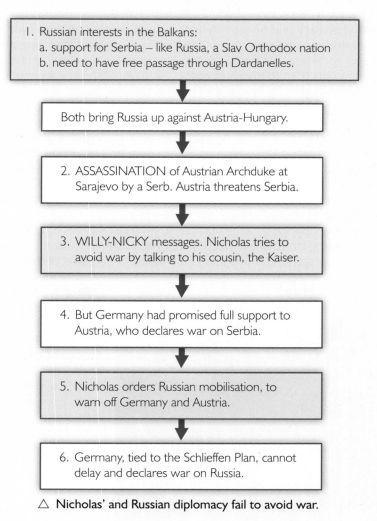

△ **Nicholas' and Russian diplomacy fail to avoid war.**

5 Why was there a revolution in February 1917?

St Petersburg was renamed **Petrograd** in 1914 because the former name sounded too 'German'. This city was central to the Revolution, see pages 86–87.

On 26 February 1917 the city of **Petrograd** was in uproar. Excited crowds thronged the streets. Soldiers with guns gathered on the corners. Barricades were built. Speakers harangued anyone who would listen. All the talk was of revolution, but everything was chaotic and uncertain.

The same day, 800 km away at Russian military headquarters at Mogilev, Tsar Nicholas II was kept informed of the deteriorating situation back in Petrograd. He had become morose, withdrawn, seemingly incapable of taking in what was happening and refusing to make any decisions. He noted in his diary that he attended Mass, wrote to his wife, went for a walk ('the weather was fine and frosty') and in the evening played dominoes. As the news got worse, his main concern was to rejoin his family in Petrograd. He ordered his train to take him home, but parts of the line were in the hands of revolutionary troops, and he only reached Pskov, still 125 km short of Petrograd. Here, on 1 March, he chain-smoked as his generals, ministers and duma leaders told him the only hope of preserving tsarism was to abdicate. On 2 March he signed an abdication document in favour of his brother Grand Duke Michael, rather than his son Alexei, aged 13. The next day Michael, who had not been consulted, refused the throne. There was no one else to take Nicholas' place. It was the end of tsarism.

In Chapter 4 you saw how, just three years earlier, the future of Russia seemed to hang on the Tsar and his decisions. By 1917 Nicholas was almost an irrelevance. By the time he abdicated, Nicholas had become a side issue to the gathering storm of a revolution that was to convulse Russia for months, even years, to come. It is this revolution which is the focus of this chapter.

The Russian people celebrated loudly. Red flags were flown, bells rang, crowds sang the old French Revolutionary anthem, the *Marseillaise*, locomotive whistles blew. Even at the battlefront, soldiers raised red flags and hung red ribbons from their rifles.

◁ **Soldiers greet the news of Nicholas' abdication.**

■ **Enquiry Focus:** Why was there a revolution in February 1917?

Here are nine reasons which may explain why there was a revolution in February 1917. Historians continue to argue about these and there is no single right answer. Your Enquiry is to decide which were the most important and identify any connections between them.

(A) Russia's performance in the First World War: Within weeks of the start of the war the Russian army suffered massive defeats. In August 1915 Nicholas took over personal command of Russian armed forces. By the end of the war 1.7 million Russians had died and Russia had suffered humiliating defeat. Tsarism as a system, and Nicholas personally, were seen to be incapable of organising and fighting a modern war.

(B) Rasputin's bad influence: With Nicholas away at the Front, Russia was effectively governed by his unpopular wife, Alexandra. Not only was she resented for her German origins, but she was deeply under the influence of the eccentric peasant holy man, Rasputin.

(D) Nicholas's refusal to make concessions: Most parties in the elected duma co-operated to offer to work with Nicholas if he would make democratic concessions. Nicholas refused.

(C) Impact of the war at home: The war had a terrible impact on the Russian people. There was rapid inflation, in which wages lagged behind prices so people were worse off, as well as shortages of food and fuel in the cities.

(F) The people: The people, especially the workers, of Petrograd came onto the streets in protest. By the end of February the city was ungovernable.

(E) The Bolsheviks: The Bolshevik Party claimed that it led the working class into the Revolution.

(H) The ruling class: The political élite blamed Nicholas for the Revolution and abandoned support for him.

(G) The soldiers: Soldiers on the streets of Petrograd refused to obey orders to put down the protest demonstrations.

(I) The peasants: In villages all over Russia peasants increasingly took over nobles' land for their own use.

Start by making your own order of significance for these reasons, using the 'diamond nine' shape below. The most important reason goes at the top, the next most important two on the second row, and so on, down to the single least important reason. These are just your initial ideas. You can adjust your order as you work through this Enquiry and find out more about each reason.

HINT: As you will remember from Chapter 3, Nicholas managed to survive the 1905 Revolution. Spotting similarities and differences between 1905 and February 1917 could help you with your enquiry. On page 83 you will be reminded and helped to do this.

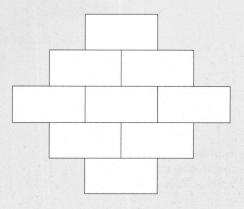

How did Russia's performance in the First World War lead to revolution?

Remind yourself of how Russia got into the **First World War** on pages 64–65.

1.7 million Russians died in the **First World War**. Hundreds of square miles of Russian territory were lost. Nicholas was humiliated by the defeats and what they revealed about the incompetence of the generals and officials he had appointed. Most of all the war brought stresses and strains to the Russian people which eventually became intolerable.

The actual declaration of war in August 1914 had produced an outburst of patriotic enthusiasm. Crowds cheered the Tsar. The duma passed a vote of loyalty to Nicholas – unanimously except for the five Bolshevik members. *The Times* correspondent in Russia wrote: *'For perhaps the first time since Napoleon's invasion of Russia* [in 1812] *the people and their Tsar were one'.* The city of St Petersburg had its German-sounding name changed to the Russian-sounding Petrograd.

Some of the 1.4 million ▷ Russians willing to die for 'Mother Russia'.

✗	Battles
→	Brusilov offensive June–Sept 1916
—	Furthest Russian advances West
—	Front line at the time of the Brest-Litovsk December negotiations, 1917
—	German penetration of Russia, March 1918
☐	Area of fighting on the Eastern front during the First World War

◁ **The Eastern Front in the First World War, 1914–17.**

The Russian army of 1.4 million men was the largest in Europe and another 4 million were called up by the end of 1914. Everyone expected the 'Russian Steamroller' to roll and so it did, making advances in the first fortnight into eastern Germany and Austria. However, the German High Command reacted quickly. They sacked their general and in a brilliant campaign, the new generals, Hindenburg and Ludendorff, defeated Russian armies at Tannenberg (August) and the Masurian Lakes (September). 170,000 Russian soldiers were killed or taken prisoner. General Samsonov, commander of the Second Army on the German Front, committed suicide.

It was clear that the Russian army had several serious disadvantages:

- Their officers were all drawn from the same narrow upper class, appointed for their loyalty to the Tsar rather than their ability. In comparison to the German officers, they were badly-trained.
- The German railway system was far better at getting troops and supplies rapidly to where they were needed. Much of the Russian railway system was single-track, so trains carrying men and supplies to the battlefront had to stop to let empty trains travelling back get past.
- Russian commanders used open radio channels to communicate with each other. German operators intercepted their messages, so knew exactly what Russian plans were.
- In contrast to the up-to-date and well-equipped German army, the Russian army was short of rifles, ammunition, artillery and shells.
- As the war went on, other shortages were revealed: boots, uniforms, winter clothing, medical supplies – everything a modern army needed. The War Minister, Sukhomlinov, was corrupt and lazy, but kept in office because Nicholas liked him and Rasputin supported him.

How did the war progress for Russia?

- **By the end of 1914** a quarter of the Russian army had been killed, wounded or taken prisoner.
- **By the end of 1915** the army had been forced into a headlong retreat of nearly 1000 km. Two million men had been killed, wounded or taken prisoner.
- **In 1916** the able General Brusilov attacked deep into Austria, but lacked supplies to sustain the advance and was forced to retreat.
- **By early 1917** there was deadlock all along the 1000 km front with no sign of an end to the war.

▽ A pile of dead Russian soldiers awaiting burial. German General Hindenburg wrote: 'The page on which the Russian losses were written has been torn out. No one knows the figure. All we know is that sometimes in our battles we had to remove the mounds of enemy corpses in order to get a clear field of fire against fresh waves of attackers.'

◁ Tsar Nicholas II arrives at Army HQ, the *Stavka*, at Mogilev.

In August 1915 Nicholas decided to take over personal command of the army (see the photograph above). This meant that he was now personally associated with any failure: no longer could his supporters argue that any problems were caused by those under him.

By the end of 1916 the army was very different from what it had been in August 1914. A large proportion of officers and men from the regular army were dead. The soldiers were peasants and workers in uniform, called up to fight for their Russian Motherland. No one could doubt their bravery and endurance. They looked after each other, were used to hardship and could virtually live off the land. However, they were beginning to question what was happening. Why did they have to wait for a comrade to be killed before they had a rifle to defend themselves with? Why were they led by officers who didn't know how to build a trench, or get attention to the wounded, or who sent them on long pointless marches, or failed to make good use of what artillery and ammunition they did have? They heard their officers muttering about getting rid of the Tsar. When they went home on leave they picked up the discontent in the villagers and the cities. By 1916 desertion was becoming a problem and there were several mutinies.

■ Review the place of Russia's performance in the First World War (Reason A on page 67) in your 'diamond nine' layout by thinking about these points:

• How did this reason contribute to the outbreak of revolution?

• How does it link to other reasons?

Make notes to justify where you've placed this reason, supporting your choice with information about how far the war helped to bring about the Revolution.

How did the actions of Rasputin contribute to the Revolution?

△ Rasputin in 1916.

Nicholas was now 800 km away from the capital – so who was left in charge? Russia was an autocracy, so all important decisions could only be taken by the Tsar. In his absence those decisions were taken by his wife, Alexandra. She was deeply unpopular: she had never got on with the Russian court and now her German background counted against her as well. Even more disturbing was her utter dependence on the extraordinary, eccentric holy man, Rasputin.

The facts of Rasputin's early life before he turned up in St Petersburg are uncertain. He was born, probably in 1869, in a peasant village in Siberia and was named Grigori Yefimovitch. As a young man he seems to have got into trouble with the law (his nickname 'Rasputin' means 'dissolute') and he took refuge in the Verkhoturye Monastery. Here he went through some kind of religious conversion, although he was not ordained as a priest and indeed was only semi-literate throughout his life. In the 1890s he lived with his wife and three children but left them in about 1901 to become a *starets* or holy man. Any number of such holy men wandered the Russian countryside, living on alms from the peasants. He developed a reputation as a powerful preacher and was taken up by influential figures in the Church in St Petersburg in 1903. The Church was losing its influence over the new urban masses and they were looking for someone to win them back. Rasputin seemed like the mythical ideal Russian peasant: simple and holy, but with mystical power.

Rasputin's arrival in St Petersburg coincided with a craze for unusual religious experiences among Russian court circles and he was taken up by several high society women. Certainly he was a striking figure, as you can see. His energy, scruffy appearance, his long hair and smelly beard, most of all his piercing eyes, captivated those who were susceptible to such things.

Whether you regard people like Rasputin as holy men, shamans or complete frauds probably depends on your religious point of view, and there are certainly equivalents in our own time. Among those who were susceptible was the Tsarina Alexandra. She had swallowed the whole tsarist story about the simple Russian peasants' attitude to the Tsar, so she loved it when Rasputin called them *'batiushka-tsar'* and *'matushka-tsarina'* ('little Father Tsar' and 'Mummy Tsarina') instead of 'Your Imperial Majesties'. But there was something more: although she had produced four beautiful daughters, their longed-for son Alexei, born in 1904, suffered from haemophilia. Moreover, she knew that she was the genetic carrier of the condition. This blood disorder is painful, life-threatening, with no known cure. The exact nature of his illness was kept a close secret. Rasputin seemed to be able to relieve Alexei's pain and even to stop the bleeding. Perhaps he did it by hypnotism, perhaps he was able to relax the boy, so the pain subsided. We would call it faith-healing. Most famously, in October 1912 Alexei was nearly dying and the doctors could do nothing. Alexandra contacted Rasputin. He replied by telegram: *'God has seen your tears and heard your prayers. Do not grieve. The little one will not die.'* And he didn't.

From then **Alexandra** was convinced Rasputin had divine powers and his influence at court knew no limits. While Nicholas was away at Army Headquarters from August 1915 onwards, Alexandra made the decisions,

One minister described **Alexandra** as having an iron will linked to not very much brain and few trusted her to make the best decisions.

often in response to Rasputin's 'dreams'. Ministers were sacked or appointed on her say-so. In eighteen months (August 1915 to February 1917), Russia had four Prime Ministers, five Ministers of the Interior, three Foreign Ministers, three War Ministers, three Transport Ministers and four Ministers of Agriculture. People bribed Rasputin with money, gifts and, sometimes, sexual favours in order to persuade him to use his influence on their behalf. In fact Rasputin seems not to have been interested in money, but he loved the power and status that he, a mere peasant, had achieved.

Rasputin was hardly the most serious problem with Nicholas' rule. However, as the scandalous rumours about him circulated, a group of nobles led by Prince Yusupov decided he had to be got rid of in order to limit the damage he was causing to tsarism. Bizarre stories surround his murder, but it seems that one night in December 1916 he was given poison, shot, beaten, tied up and thrown into the river. Even then the post mortem reported that he had water in his lungs, so must have been breathing as he hit the icy water.

Rasputin was so close to the Tsar by 1916 that the attack on him was virtually an attack on the Tsar. It was a sign, if Nicholas was prepared to heed it, that even the tight group of court aristocrats were turning against him.

■ Review your diamond nine layout on page 67. Where does Rasputin (Reason B) belong as a reason for the February 1917 Revolution?

Can you explain your decision?

△ Rasputin seems to have been a follower of a religious sect called *Kylysty*, who believed that those who sin more, repent more and so are more holy. Their rituals involved dancing naked, flagellation and group sex. Rasputin was well-known in St Petersburg for his alcohol-fuelled sex orgies. It is extremely unlikely that he and Alexandra were lovers, but postcards like this one were circulating freely in Petrograd in 1916 and did great damage not only to her reputation but to tsarism as a system.

■ Does Rasputin matter? The lurid stories on this page may not all be true but what can you infer from them about life at the Russian court in 1915–16?

How did the impact of the war at home contribute to revolution?

This is Reason C on your list on page 67. Before you begin reading, remind yourself of where you put this reason in your diamond nine.

During the First World War, the British Prime Minister, David Lloyd George, described modern war as 'total war'. By this he meant that war is no longer just about soldiers; governments now have to ensure the welfare of the people at home, so that they continue to support the war and work to provide all the supplies that the armed forces need. What impact did the war have at home in the villages, towns and cities of Russia?

Inflation

Between the outbreak of war in July 1914 and early 1917 prices rose over 300 per cent. This inflation began because government expenditure increased from 4 million to 30 million roubles a year in order to pay for the war. At the same time government income fell because of the war:

- 30 per cent of government revenue had come from the tax on alcohol but Nicholas had banned the manufacture of vodka to keep Russians sober for the war effort.
- The war cut foreign trade, reducing significantly the government's income from taxes on exported goods. Before the war, half of Russia's exports had gone to Germany and these now ceased completely. In addition, it was now impossible to export goods through the Dardanelles to the outside world (see map on page 64) because Turkey's entry into the war on Germany's side meant that that route was blocked.

The government tried to make up for the fall in income by printing more and more paper money, but this caused steep inflation. Wages rose by 100 per cent but this was a long way short of the inflation in prices, which particularly affected everyday necessities such as food. This decline in living standards led to widespread hardship and anger.

Shortages

Not only had prices risen fast, but there were shortages of basic items in the cities, especially bread. By 1916 only a third of the food and fuel the people of Petrograd and Moscow required was getting to these great cities. There were two factors causing these shortages:

a) **Breakdown of the railway system:** The effort to keep an army of millions supplied was more than the Russian railway system could cope with. Engines ran out of coal. Signalling systems broke down, so trains could not move. Single track railways meant trains blocked each other. Food rotted in the immobile wagons.

b) **Grain supply from the peasants:** By 1916, 20 per cent less grain was reaching markets than in 1914. There were several reasons for this. With so many men called up into the army, many peasant farms were short of farmhands. Many farm horses had been also requisitioned for army use. At the same time peasants were reluctant to send grain to market. Why sell your grain when there was nothing worth buying because of rising prices and shortages of consumer goods?

Impact of shortages on the peasants

It was their sons who were getting killed. In addition, they were struggling with fewer hands and fewer horses to farm the land. There were shortages of the few things they couldn't do without: sugar, paraffin, matches. Grain prices were high, but so were prices of anything they might want to buy. With rising discontent the **old grievances** about land re-emerged. In 1916, there were 300 outbreaks of peasant attacks on nobles' houses and property, 90 of which had to be put down by the army.

See pages 34–35 to remind yourself about what peasants' **old grievances** were.

Impact of shortages on the workers

War industries were pulling thousands of workers into the factories so there was a big increase in the urban population. Living and working conditions in Russian cities were already poor (see pages 36–37) and they now became intolerable. Factory owners drove their workers hard to meet wartime production targets. Hours increased, industrial injuries became more frequent. By 1916 the number of strikes was rising fast, and the proportion with political aims was rising even faster. Then came the winter of 1916–17 which was especially cold. Every day people spent long hours queuing for food in freezing conditions, often to go home empty-handed and hungry.

How did the war affect the Russian people?

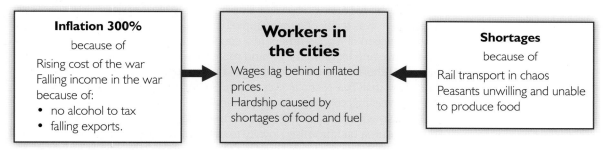

> Review your diamond nine layout on page 67. Where does the impact of the war at home (Reason C) belong as a reason for the February 1917 Revolution?
> - Can you explain your decision?
> - How does it link to other reasons?

Why was bread important?

Bread is really important to the Russians. Even today, the average Russian eats three times more bread than a Western European. In the early twentieth century it was even more important, making up the bulk of every meal. A Russian worker in 1900 ate up to 1 kilo of bread a day. This was usually 'black bread' made from rye or a mixture of rye and wheat. When times were hard and other food expensive or unavailable, bread was essential. Without it the Russian people starved.

Nicholas' refusal to make concessions

The **Kadets** were the Constitutional Democrats (KDs). They were formed in 1905 with support from the middle classes. They supported the growth of liberal democracy and opposed revolution.

On 1 November 1916, Paul Miliukov, leader of the **Kadets** (and a history teacher!), made a powerful speech in the duma. Here is an extract.

> We now see that we can no more legislate with this government than we can lead Russia to victory with it. When the Duma declares again and again that the Home Front must be organised for a successful war, and the government continues to insist that to organise the country means to organise revolution, … is this stupidity or treason? [Voices from the left: 'Treason!']
>
> We have many reasons for being discontented with this government, but all these reasons boil down to one general one: the incompetence and evil intentions of the present government. And therefore in the name of the millions of victims and their spilled blood, we shall fight until we get a responsible government which is in agreement with the general principles of our programme. A Cabinet which does not satisfy these conditions does not deserve the confidence of the Duma and should go! [Cries of 'Bravo!' and loud and prolonged applause]

Why was this speech important? Remember that in 1907 Stolypin (see page 56) manipulated the voting system to ensure a more docile duma. Yet here is this docile duma applauding a speaker who questions whether the Tsar's government was guilty of either 'stupidity or treason'. These views would be a strong criticism of a government in a country with free speech. In tsarist Russia it was brave and extraordinary – and more than that, it was an important step towards Nicholas' downfall. Miliukov and his supporters had come to the conclusion that Tsar Nicholas was stupid. So what did they mean by 'stupid' and why was this conclusion so important?

To begin with we have to go back to the outbreak of war in August 1914. Then the duma had promised loyalty to the Tsar and happily agreed to be sent home so the Tsar's ministers could get on with running the war. However, it soon became clear what a mess they were making of it. Unable to support the war effort by working with the government, many able people created their own organisations. For example, leading businessmen set up the War Industries Committee to co-ordinate production of war matériel. They were more successful than the government, who tended to give contracts to their cronies. Other organisations outside the Tsar's direct control were the *Zemstvo* Union and the Union of Town Councils. They combined their efforts in a joint body called *Zemgor*. By 1916 *Zemgor* was employing 55,000 people, providing medical supplies and hospital care. It was organised by Prince Lvov, an able and hard-working man and a loyal supporter of tsarism. These non-governmental organisations were democratically-elected and gave opportunities for liberals, the middle classes and business leaders to meet. Inevitably they contrasted their success with the government's efforts.

The Tsar reluctantly allowed the duma to reconvene in June 1915. Faced with his unwillingness to listen to them, in August 1915 the Octobrists (see page 57), the Kadets and others combined to form the Progressive Bloc. They called for the usual moderate, liberal programme – free speech, control of the secret police, recognition of the rights of minorities, especially Poles, Finns and

Jews. Most of all, however, they wanted ministers to be members of the duma and to be chosen because they were competent enough to command its support. (This is the 'programme' Miliukov was referring to in his speech, above.) They appealed to the Tsar to co-operate with them and form a 'government of national confidence', to work together to win the war – and avoid revolution.

Nicholas' ministers dared not try to persuade him to make any concessions. Alexandra also encouraged him to resist, suggesting he should comb his hair with Rasputin's comb in order to pick up some of his strength. She regarded the Progressive Bloc as *Fiends … who need smacking'.*

The Tsar therefore rejected out of hand the appeal from the Progressive Bloc. He saw it simply as the first stage towards democracy, which he was determined to resist. Miliukov said the government *'brushed aside the hand that was offered to them'.* A tsarist deputy, Shulgin, tried in vain to point out that *'the whole purpose of the Progressive Bloc was to prevent revolution'.* So there was more to Miliukov's speech than just the anger of competent, democratic politicians watching an incompetent government lead their country to defeat. There is the anger of seeing the huge war casualties – the *'millions of victims and their spilled blood'.* There is the frustration of recognising that the Tsar's government are incapable of winning the war or governing the country – or preventing the revolution they feared.

The Tsar was too blinded by his own prejudices to see it, but these progressives were moderates, not revolutionaries. They were men of wealth, of property and business. They feared revolution because they had a lot to lose. Miliukov's answer to his own question 'stupidity or treason' is that he thought the Tsar and his ministers were stupid, not treasonous, for not seeing that he and his colleagues in the duma were his best hope for avoiding revolution. This was the end of the line for Miliukov and the Progressive Bloc. From then on the liberal duma politicians began to see that Nicholas had to go.

> ■ Review your diamond nine layout on page 67. Where does Nicholas' refusal to make concessions (Reason D) go as a reason for the February 1917 Revolution? You may find it useful to think about how important the concessions Nicholas made in the October Manifesto (1905) were in enabling Nicholas to survive the 1905 revolution.
>
> Can you explain your decision?
>
> How does it link to other reasons?

Looking back … looking ahead.

So far we have seen how the first four reasons (A–D), war and its impact coupled with the attitudes of Tsar Nicholas, had produced anger, suffering and bitterness – but not a revolution. Do you think that by early 1917 revolution was possible or likely?

I think that Reason A, Russia's performance in the war, certainly made revolution likely. It was not just that the defeats hit Nicholas' own prestige. For the first year of the war, defeat could be put down to bad generals and ministers, but from August 1915 Nicholas himself took command and things got no better. Ordinary soldiers knew that it was not that they were cowardly – in fact they were astonishingly brave. They could see it was the incompetence and inadequacy of their government. And when they went home on leave their stories ran round the village or the city quarter they came from.

Where did you put Reason B, Rasputin? Maybe it lowered Nicholas' reputation even further, but Nicholas' reputation was already pretty low. I think the interesting thing is that it was powerful courtiers who bumped him off, not revolutionary workers. Those who had most to lose if tsarism fell were getting worried.

In my opinion, Reason C, the impact of war at home, is probably the most important so far. By early 1917 many people in Russia, particularly in the cities, were driven to desperation by hunger, hardship and cold.

Reason D marks a further step down the road to revolution. Nicholas was too stupid to see it, but he had rejected the kind of people who had saved him in 1905. His attitude moved revolution from 'possible' to 'likely'.

The word 'likely' has been used a lot, but a revolution being 'likely' is not at all the same as a revolution breaking out. What was it, then, which brought about the February Revolution?

The outbreak of revolution, February 1917

The photographer's caption to this photo says it was taken during the 'first day' of the February Revolution. If that is true, these are the people who brought it about. How can this photograph help us with our Enquiry?
Look closely at the picture. It seems to be a street scene, with trams in the background. We could check whether these trams were in use in Petrograd in 1917 and so help to authenticate the place and date.

Most of the people are women, on the right and all down the street. They are not young and are simply dressed, in dark clothes, with headscarves. Their banners say:

> Increase the rations of the families of soldiers, the defenders of freedom and world peace.

> Feed the children of the defenders of the homeland.

In among them are some soldiers, most clearly on the left, waving cheerfully. Then in the foreground are some younger people, boys and girls, some smiling at the camera. And then there is the well-dressed man in a bowler hat, front left. He may be middle class, but better paid workers did like to dress smartly.

From this photograph you get a sense of the power of the people on the streets of Petrograd. There is also the feeling that different groups are coming together, realising that they share grievances: the women are short of food, especially for the children, but support the soldiers, who in turn support them. It is not at all violent, but neither are they going to go home quietly. They don't look like natural revolutionaries, so it must have taken a lot for them to protest in this way – and they probably won't be easily subdued, either.

The February Revolution day by day

The February Revolution happened over just nine days. Here is a diary of some key events each day.

February 22	A series of bitter strikes at the huge Putilov Arms factory in Petrograd about wages, hours and rising prices culminates in a lock-out by the employers. Thousands of angry workers are now on the streets, along with women protesting about food and fuel shortages.
February 23	International Women's Day demonstrators are joined by many strikers. Soldiers reluctant to use force against demonstrators.
February 24	Strikes spread throughout Petrograd and beyond; more factories occupied by workers; more food riots.
February 25	General strike brings Petrograd to a standstill. Workers demand food and an end to the war. General Khabalov, the general in charge of Petrograd, reports that some soldiers are defecting to the demonstrators.
February 26	Nicholas orders the army to put down the demonstrations. Troops still loyal to the government fire on demonstrators and 50 are killed.
February 27	Mutiny of many Petrograd garrisons. Strikers seize rifles, open the prisons. Remaining loyal troops attacked.
	Petrograd Soviet of Workers, Sailors and Soldiers Deputies formed. Meets in the Tauride Palace, the same building where the duma meets.
	Nicholas orders dissolution of the duma, but some members refuse to depart and instead form a Provisional Committee.
February 28	Virtually all soldiers in Petrograd now join the revolution. Nicholas tries to return to Petrograd, but is stopped by railway workers and mutinous troops.
March 1	Mutiny spreads to Moscow and the naval base at Kronstadt.
March 2	Duma Provisional Committee appoints ministers and declares itself the Provisional Government of Russia.
	A group of generals and duma members advise Nicholas that as he has lost the support of the army he should abdicate. Nicholas agrees to abdicate in favour of his brother Michael.

The result of these events is known as Dual Power: the Provisional Government, based on the old *duma*, and the Soviet, elected by factory and, soon, army committees.

■ This page helps you place factors E–H in your diamond nine.

■ What evidence is there in the diary on page 79 of the role of the soldiers in the Revolution? Where would you place them in your diamond?

For this section it would be useful to look back at the views of different groups of historians on pages 22–23.

Be cautious about this table: it is based on his examination of police records. We have to ask whether the police were the best people to decide whether a strike was 'political' or 'economic'.

Who led the Revolution?

The diary on page 79 is a simplification of what was actually going on. Real events were confused and fast-moving. Thousands of people took part, each for their own reasons. Clearly the real revolution arose out of strikes about down-to-earth issues: wages, hours, working conditions, the price and scarcity of food. But what were the big causal factors which drove the Revolution? Different historians have explained these events in different ways. Soviet historians have started with their own ideas about the story they want to tell and selected the evidence which supports it. Other historians have been driven by the sources they have had to work from.

The army

In any revolution the allegiance of the soldiers is crucial. In 1905 most of the troops stayed loyal to the Tsar; in February 1917 they threw in their lot with the protesting workers. Why? The incompetence of their officers and the failures of supplies have been explained on pages 69 and 71. But issues of the right to life and human dignity came into it, too. By early March soldiers' committees had been set up in many regiments. Almost everywhere they removed the officers they hated, the bullies and petty tyrants, and replaced them with officers they respected.

Peasants

For all their anger at the war and its impact on their lives, February was not an important phase in the peasant revolution. Unrest, land seizures and attacks on landowners' property continued, but peaked later in the year.

Bolsheviks, workers or the ruling class?

From soon after 1917, Soviet historians set out to show that the February Revolution was a rising of the proletariat (the industrial workers) because this was the pattern Marx had laid out. Soviet historians made much of the experience of the workers, asserting that by 1917 more than half the workers in Petrograd had taken part in the 1905 revolution and the strikes of 1912–14. Their case is that it was these workers, influenced by the Bolsheviks, who led the demand for a revolution to put an end to tsarism. The number of workers in Petrograd had been swollen during the war by an influx from the villages to work in the war industries, but these more inexperienced workers usually only made economic demands such as better pay and working conditions. This table, from the work of the Soviet historian I.P. Leiberov, published in the 1970s, suggests that in 1916 political strikes were slightly fewer, but bigger, involving far more workers than economic strikes, so the political revolution was getting nearer.

Political Strikes 1916	Number of strikers	Economic strikes 1916	Number of strikers
330	377,421	354	243,500

At the same time Soviet historians also insisted that it was the Bolshevik Party which guided these workers, giving them ideas and slogans to use in their protests. Soviet historians have contended that, despite the efforts of the *Okhrana* to break them up, the Bolsheviks had organisations in 200 towns and cities as well as in garrisons and naval bases. They claim 115 cells in Petrograd, with 3000 members, 2500 of whom were workers. Two million copies of leaflets were in circulation. Lenin was in close and regular touch with Bolshevik members through his newsletter, *Social Democrat*. These arguments then led Soviet historians to claim that it was the Bolsheviks who led the workers away from down-to-earth issues towards political change: the removal of the Tsar, democracy, worker participation in running factories. They also claim that it was Bolshevik ideas which spilled over to the soldiers, especially those who were garrisoned near solidly proletarian areas of the city, and encouraged them to disobey orders to shoot the protesting workers.

> ■ Where would Soviet historians place the workers and the Bolsheviks in the diamond nine?

In contrast, western historians of the Cold War years played down the role of the workers on the streets and the role of the Bolsheviks. They insist that the workers' protests were merely a response to the failure of food supplies due to the chaos of war. In a book published in 1955, the American historian Leonard Schapiro described the demonstrators as *'an anarchical mob ... with no thought but destruction'*. They argue that the soldiers in Petrograd mutinied because they were afraid of being sent to the front line. These historians point out that, in the end, Nicholas abdicated, not because of street protests, but on the advice of the ruling élite – generals, ministers and duma leaders.

However, historians in the west had to rely largely on the memoirs of Russians who had been driven out of Russia by the Bolsheviks after the October Revolution. These were mostly members of other parties and claimed that Russia in 1914 was becoming a real democracy. (We explored this interpretation in Chapter 4.) The western historians' argument is that Nicholas proved totally incapable of giving the leadership required by the war and relied on a series of incompetents as ministers. He then took the disastrous decision in August 1915 to go to Army Headquarters, leaving too much power in the hands of Alexandra and Rasputin. He foolishly rejected the offer of co-operation from the Progressive Bloc, thus losing the support of loyal moderates. Their view is that the end came when the ruling class told Nicholas he had to go; it was nothing to do with protests on the streets.

> ■ Where would western historians place workers, Bolsheviks and the ruling class on the diamond nine?

However, by concentrating on the political élite, these western historians missed the point. The ruling élite only advised Nicholas to abdicate because, by February, power lay with the people on the streets. They wouldn't have advised abdication if they hadn't felt threatened by that power. It's important to realise that the people on the streets were not just a mob, bent on looting. They were ordinary Russians, like the people we can see in the photo on page 78, driven beyond the point of endurance by hunger, cold, poverty and the age-old uncaring contempt of their masters. None were present at Pskov when Nicholas gave up the throne, but the fact was that by then the people controlled Petrograd, not the tsarist government. This was the real revolution, and it was to continue through 1917. On the streets, Nicholas' abdication changed little.

However, this argument doesn't mean that Soviet historians were right in saying that the workers were led and shaped by the Bolsheviks. From the 1980s, new historians have examined the lives and beliefs of ordinary people in factories and regiments. They looked to see how far both the Soviet and the liberal view were actually supported by the evidence. What have these historians to tell us from their research?

These revisionist historians argue that the influence of the Bolsheviks in February was not great. The figures for Bolshevik Party membership have probably been exaggerated by Soviet historians. The existence of lots of newsletters and leaflets doesn't mean that lots of people read them. It is hard to pin down the influence of the Bolsheviks: if demonstrators carry a banner with a Bolshevik slogan, does that make them all Bolsheviks? Soviet historians had played down the influence of other parties, and carried out little research about them. Membership of the SRs, even in Petrograd, was probably larger than the Bolsheviks at this stage. This may seem strange, as the SRs were a peasant-based party, but many workers were fresh from the villages – in fact 20 per cent of them still owned some land in a village. Some idea of real Bolshevik influence at this stage can be seen from the fact that, of 242 workers' soviets formed by the end of March, the Bolsheviks only controlled 27, and only about 40 of the 600 or so deputies in the Petrograd Soviet in March were Bolsheviks.

The revisionists' other major point is about leadership: Lenin was in Switzerland and hadn't visited Russia for ten years, Trotsky was in New York and other key Bolshevik leaders were also in exile. The events of February took them completely by surprise. The demonstrators did pick up Bolshevik slogans, but that was surely because they meant something to them. It may not fit anyone's pre-formed theories; the February Revolution was, as the historian W.H. Chamberlin observed as long ago as 1935:

■ Who would the revisionists place at the top of the diamond?

One of the most leaderless, spontaneous, anonymous revolutions of all time.

Comparing 1905 and 1917

Before deciding on the final arrangement of your diamond nine, let's look at why the February 1917 Revolution succeeded while the 1905 Revolution did not. What was similar and what was different? What can we learn from these similarities and differences? And did any of the participants in 1917 learn anything from 1905? If so, what?

	1905	1917
WAR	Defeat in the Russo–Japanese War in 1904–05 was a symbol of tsarist incompetence and one of the triggers of the Revolution. The war was fought far away and was over by September 1905.	The First World War had a far greater impact than the Russo–Japanese War. Russian soldiers were fighting on Russian territory and it had been going on for over three and a half years by February 1917. The massive loss of life brought grief and resentment to thousands of families. Continuing defeats and the loss of huge amounts of territory hit the Tsar's prestige. The badly-trained officers, the generals who owed their position to the favour of the Tsar rather than their ability, the collapse of support to the frontline forces, all revealed far more: the utter failure of tsarist government. The impact of the war on civilians was equally important, with hunger and desperation bringing people onto the streets in protest.
OPPOSITION	Liberals, workers and peasants all demanded change.	Liberals and moderates hoped that the abdication of the Tsar would prevent a real revolution. However, many peasants and workers were determined not to be robbed of their aims as they had been in 1905, but to carry out their own revolution.
SOLDIERS	Most of the army stayed loyal to the Tsar.	By February 1917 most of the regular army had been killed and the armed forces were now made up of conscripts. They were the workers and peasants of Russia, now in uniform, and reflected their deep discontent. They had experienced the incompetence (and often the contempt) of their officers, and the lack of organised support from the Tsar's government. At crucial moments they refused to fire on protesting workers and joined the Revolution themselves.
MINISTERS	Nicholas had able advisers – Witte and Stolypin.	Nicholas dismissed Witte in 1906 and Stolypin was assassinated in 1911. After them, Nicholas appointed nonentities, too fond of their own positions, and too aware that they would be instantly dismissed if they dared to give him advice he didn't like. After he left for the Front in August 1915, matters, if anything, got worse under the combined ineptitude of Rasputin and Alexandra.
CONCESSIONS	Nicholas made concessions in the October Manifesto.	The 1905 October Manifesto won over the liberals and gave Nicholas the space to crush the opposition. While workers and peasants of 1917 remembered this lesson from 1905, Nicholas did not, and rejected the offer of co-operation from the 'Progressive Bloc' in the duma.

■ Concluding your Enquiry

1 Several reasons from page 67 have now come together. Where have you placed: The Bolsheviks (Reason E), the people (Reason F), the soldiers (Reason G), the ruling class (Reason H) and the peasants (Reason I)? What are your reasons for your judgement of their significance as reasons for the Revolution of February 1917?

2 Finalise your diamond nine layout. Think carefully about links between the nine factors before reaching your conclusion.

Lenin (1870–1924)

'An unmitigated disaster for the human race.'

'The monster who sired the evils of our time.'

These quotations are from two western historians about Lenin. Meanwhile, in the **USSR** Lenin was a hero: the great city of St Petersburg was re-named Leningrad on his death in 1924. Twenty other towns took his name. Posters like this one, statues and paintings appeared everywhere. His embalmed body can be seen in his mausoleum in Red Square, Moscow.

All these over-the-top portrayals hinder rather than help us in trying to understand this man whose actions will play such a large part in the last two enquiries in this book.

So what do we actually know about Lenin?

Vladimir Ilyich Ulyanov, as he was called until he took his revolutionary nickname, was born in 1870. His father was a Chief Inspector of Schools, a senior civil servant with the right to be addressed as 'Your Excellency'. Young Vladimir did well at school but showed no interest in politics. Then, in 1887, his eldest brother Alexander took part in a plot to assassinate Tsar Alexander III. He was arrested and executed. This seems to have radicalised the 17-year-old Vladimir. He began to read political literature and joined opposition groups at university. He was arrested in 1895, serving fourteen months in solitary confinement before being exiled to Siberia. There he met other revolutionaries and changed his name to Lenin. He was joined in exile by Nadezhda Krupskaya, who became his wife and lifelong support. When his term of exile ended in 1900 he went abroad, living in various cities in western Europe including London. He was entirely absent from Russia for the next seventeen years, apart from a few months during the 1905–06 Revolution, in which he took no real part.

What did he believe? At first Lenin turned to the Populists, like his brother. Although, like many late nineteenth century Russian radicals, he later moved on to Marx, Populist belief in 'the people', and in the need for violent action to force change stayed with him all his life, and influenced his Marxism. This distinguished him from more orthodox Marxists, like the Mensheviks, who believed that history itself would bring about revolution – eventually.

△ A poster glorifying Lenin as a hero, with firm jaw, commanding eyes and active pose. The text says 'Long live the Soviet Revolution'.

USSR
Union of Soviet Socialist Republics. Russia and 14 other Communist states which was set up in 1922 and dissolved in 1991

Lenin's name
Several revolutionaries, changed their names, partly to confuse the *Okhrana* and partly to put their old identity behind them. Lenin is thought to have taken his name from the River Lena, which political prisoners had to cross on their way to Siberia.

Both his enemies and his worshippers like to portray him as a master-planner, creating the Bolshevik Party, leading it relentlessly towards their seizure of power in October 1917. Certainly he split with the rest of the Russian Social Democrat Party in 1902–03 (see page 44) over what kind of party it ought to be. Firstly, he was serious about revolution: he was determined that the Party should be more than an intellectual discussion group. Secondly, it had to be centralised and tightly-controlled. The Mensheviks were for a looser, more open party, but Lenin felt that to resist infiltration by the Tsar's police, the *Okhrana*, the Bolsheviks had to be much more disciplined. However, with nearly a quarter of a million members by late 1917, the Bolshevik Party was quite open and impossible to control: the Central Committee could give instructions, but could not force local branches to comply with them.

Nor is it true that he never made any mistakes. As you will see, he nearly wrecked everything in the July Days (see page 99). And he seems to have had no detailed plans at all for what to do once the proletarian revolution had taken place, but believed that Russia would automatically move into the utopia shown as Stage 5 in the diagram of Marxism on page 21. In fact, far from being a master-planner, with a blueprint for revolution worked out back in 1902, he was a master-improviser, reading situations as they developed and deciding what had to be done at that moment. This is what he did when he arrived at the **Finland Station** in April 1917, again in October 1917, then over the growing Civil War in summer 1918, and finally in 1921 over the New Economic Policy (NEP).

In 1869 the radical agitator Nechaev described what a revolutionary had to be like:

> A revolutionary is a dedicated man. He has no personal feelings … Everything in him is subordinated towards a single thought and a single passion – the revolution.

Many have applied Nechaev's characterisation to Lenin. He was indeed dedicated to the cause of revolution, and lived a simple life, even when he was ruler of Russia. He got his own way in the long, rowdy meetings by sheer force of personality and was ruthless in outmanoeuvring his opponents. He was intolerant of those who did not agree with him, abusing them, calling them 'blockheads', 'scum', 'stupid hens' – and worse. Once in power, he was quite prepared to order the death of his enemies. John Reed, an American communist who knew Lenin, described his charismatic power:

> A strange popular leader—a leader purely by virtue of intellect; colourless, humourless, uncompromising and detached—but with the power of explaining profound ideas in simple terms, of analysing a concrete situation. And combined with shrewdness, the greatest intellectual audacity.

Yet when the passion was over, the sleepless nights and hyperactivity passed; he would crumble, and Krupskaya would take him into the country to rest and recover.

Finland Station
Railway station in Petrograd for trains to and from Finland

In the first Enquiry (Chapter 3) you were asked to think whether history is made by single important individuals, or by other forces. Now, apply this to Lenin. In other words, did he bring about the Russian Revolution?

At some point as you read the two Enquiries in Chapters 6 and 7, you should try to decide what you think about this issue.

Petrograd: the city at the heart of the Revolution

We should never forget that Russia consists of thousands of villages and hundreds of towns and cities. But all the big events of the 1917 Revolution which are at the centre of Chapters 5 and 6 took place in Petrograd, so knowing something about the city is important.

Tsar Peter the Great ruled Russia from 1682 to 1725 and wanted to give his country a much more westward-looking, European outlook. Among his many changes was the building of a new capital city on the River Neva, with access to the Baltic Sea and so to northern Europe, where he had travelled and found so much to admire. The city was called after him, St Petersburg. When the First World War began, its name was changed to the Russian version – 'Petrograd'. On Lenin's death in 1924 it was renamed Leningrad, until, in 1991, the city reverted to its original name: St Petersburg.

△ St Petersburg was planned by Tsar Peter and built in a unified European classical style. The magnificent buildings of the centre of the city have made it a UNESCO World Heritage Site. The river and canals divide up the city, as this picture of grand buildings on the Griboyedov Canal shows.

Map of Petrograd in 1917

Vyborg District: An area of heavy industry, terrible overcrowded housing and endemic disease. Notice that a single bridge links Vyborg with the rest of the city: control of this bridge could prevent, or allow, Vyborg workers into the city.

Notice also that the Finland Station, where Lenin arrived in April 1917, is in this working class district.

Tauride Palace: The Provisional Government <u>and</u> the Petrograd Soviet met here (see photographs on pages 90 and 92).

Vasilevsky Island: An area of industry and workers housing.

Battleship *Aurora*: On the night of 25 October 1917 a blank shot from this battleship was the signal for the Bolsheviks to take over the city.

Smolny Institute: Bolshevik headquarters.

Nevsky Prospekt: Main shopping street and route of many demonstrations.

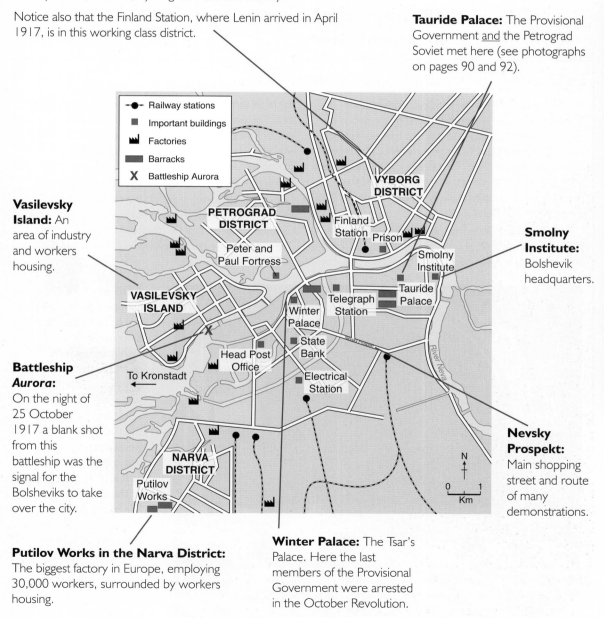

Putilov Works in the Narva District: The biggest factory in Europe, employing 30,000 workers, surrounded by workers housing.

Winter Palace: The Tsar's Palace. Here the last members of the Provisional Government were arrested in the October Revolution.

The October Revolution: rising of the masses or *coup d'état*?

48 hours that changed the world – two interpretations

The Soviet view: 'The Great October Socialist Revolution'

On 24 October 1917, the Bolshevik leaders at the Smolny Institute in Petrograd, inspired by the genius of Lenin's leadership, laid preparations to take power and form the first popular Marxist government in the world. During the night of 24/25 October, dedicated Red Guard units, with Bolshevik sailors and soldiers, seized key points in the city: bridges, railway stations, the telephone exchange, the power station.

The Provisional Government was still meeting in the Winter Palace. At 9.40 pm on the evening of 25 October the battle cruiser *Aurora*, which had been taken over by Bolshevik sailors and moved nearer the city, fired a blank shot. This was the signal for a heroic storming of the Winter Palace by hundreds of Red Guards and Bolshevik workers, who arrested the last remnants of the Provisional Government.

The day after the October Revolution, Leon Trotsky, Commissar for Foreign Affairs in the new Bolshevik government, described how he saw what had just happened: *'The rising of the masses of the people needs no justification ... The masses followed our banner and our insurrection was victorious.'*

◁ A still from the film *Oktober*, directed by the brilliant Soviet director Sergei Eisenstein, which portrays this version of events. This film was made for the tenth anniversary of the October Revolution in 1927. It is sometimes shown as if it is a newsreel of the actual events. Far more people took part in the film than were there in 1917, and the film-making caused more damage to the building than the actual Revolution did!

The western historians' view: '*A coup d'état* by armed conspirators'

This interpretation says that the Provisional Government was too inexperienced to solve all Russia's problems and meet people's impossible expectations. Lenin and his dedicated little band of followers plotted to seize power. The Bolsheviks had no mass support, but Lenin saw their opportunity and sent a small contingent of armed men to remove the Provisional Government.

Richard Pipes, History Professor at Harvard University in the USA wrote, in 1992: '*October was not a revolution but a classic* **coup d'état***, planned in the dead of night*'. Orlando Figes, British Historian, wrote in 1996: '*It was a coup d'état actively supported by a small minority of the population.*'

> See pages 22–23 for a summary of the views of different groups of historians.

Coup d'état
the forced removal of a government, usually by a small armed group

■ Enquiry Focus: Rising of the masses or *coup d'état*?

The job of the historian is to make order out of the chaos, to find the patterns. The trouble is that different people find different patterns. To Trotsky, this was clearly '*... a rising of the masses*' but western historians didn't see the October Revolution like that at all. As you can see, both Richard Pipes and Orlando Figes have described the events of October 1917 as a *coup d'état*.

Now it's your turn.

We need to look over the eight months from February to October to see the pattern of rise and fall of popularity and power. Lifeline A is a suggestion of the pattern of support for the Bolsheviks through these eight months. Your task will be to decide:

- whether you think the pattern is correct
- why it rises and falls at those times.

If it is correct, then the Bolsheviks did have massive popular support by October, and Trotsky was right. If you disagree, and the Bolsheviks had no real popular support, then western historians like Richard Pipes are right.

Lifeline B will be up to you. Draw the lifeline of support for the Provisional Government and explain the shape you have chosen. Will your Lifeline B suggest that the Provisional Government had lost popular support by October?

This enquiry is divided into three sections and you will review your lifelines at the end of each section:

1 Early March – mid-June: The window of opportunity
2 Mid-June – End of September: Kerensky's mistakes
3 October: Lenin seizes the moment

At the end you will make your own judgement about what you think really happened in Petrograd in October 1917.

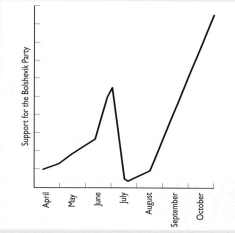

△ Lifeline A: Support for the Bolsheviks during 1917.

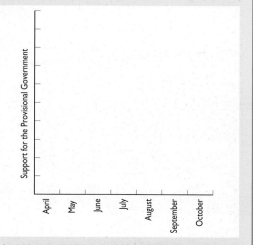

△ Lifeline B: Support for the Provisional Government during 1917.

1: Early March–mid-June: the window of opportunity

Could the Provisional Government win popular support?

The February Revolution settled nothing. There was an atmosphere of euphoria, but the real revolution was only just beginning. The problems that had led to the Revolution in the first place had not gone away.

Everyone had high hopes for a better life – better wages, cheaper and more plentiful food, shorter working hours, better housing, more polite bosses, equality for women, democracy, the rule of law … And that was just in Petrograd. Similar revolutions soon took place in Moscow and other cities. On the front line, some soldiers wanted immediate peace, others wanted to fight on, but defensively, protecting their motherland from further invasion. Peasants were wondering whether this was the moment to seize the land they always claimed was theirs because they had toiled on it. In Poland and Finland, Georgia and the Ukraine, nationalists proclaimed their right to independence.

Who could give these people what they wanted? On 2 March several leading duma politicians declared a Provisional Government. Provisional means temporary: they intended to run the country until proper elections could be held for a democratic government. They had the support of landowners, army officers, factory owners and middle class intellectuals and met in the Tauride Palace.

▽ The Tauride Palace today. Here, the First Duma met in 1906, both assemblies of the 'Dual Power' met in 1917, as well as the short-lived Constituent Assembly in January 1918 (see Chapter 7).

In another huge room in the Tauride Palace, another body was already meeting: the Petrograd **Soviet**. This started on 27 February as a meeting of workers elected from each factory, as well as a number of socialist intellectuals. Two days later delegates elected by soldiers' committees requested to join the Soviet.

Soviet
A meeting of elected representatives of workers and soldiers

The situation at this point is sometimes called 'Dual Power', with two bodies, the Provisional Government and the Petrograd Soviet, existing side by side.

The Provisional Government really appointed itself. It was made up of those members of the duma who had tried to persuade Nicholas to make democratic reforms in 1916 – mainly Kadets and the Progressive Bloc (see pages 76–77). The most well-known was Paul Miliukov, Foreign Minister, and the new Prime Minister was Prince Lvov. Lvov came from an old Russian aristocratic family, but had become widely respected for his war work. As chair of *Zemgor* (town and district councils – see page 76) he had worked tirelessly to organise supplies and medical assistance for the troops to fill the gap left by the incompetence of the tsarist government officials.

What right did these former duma members have to rule? They had been among those elected to the duma in 1912, but as we saw on page 57, these elections were held on an extremely restricted franchise, in which property-owners had by far the greatest influence. Nevertheless, it was a claim of sorts and anyway, the new government was only 'Provisional'– to run the country until proper elections could be held.

On a wave of goodwill and revolutionary enthusiasm, when complete strangers hugged each other in the street, the Provisional Government had a window of opportunity to show if it could meet people's expectations and gain popular support.

The freest country in the world

The Provisional Government set about creating a classic liberal democracy:

- The hated tsarist secret police, the *Okhrana*, was abolished. Political prisoners were released. Press censorship was abolished.
- All men and women over twenty years old had the right to vote. (This made it the widest franchise in the world at the time.)
- Trade unions were legalised. Workers had a guaranteed eight-hour day.
- All discrimination on the grounds of race, gender or belief was illegal.

Having carried out their political revolution, most of the members of the Provisional Government had gone about as far as they wanted to go. But these political changes did little to address the demands of the soldiers, peasants and workers for social and economic change.

Why didn't the Soviet take power?

In many ways the Petrograd Soviet had more right to take power. A soviet of workers' representatives had been set up during the 1905 Revolution, and some Mensheviks encouraged workers to form a similar organisation in 1917. It started as a meeting of delegates elected by their factory committees, but workers were soon outnumbered by soldiers elected by their comrades. With soviet meetings attended by up to 3000 people, decision-making was impossible so an Executive Committee was set up, mainly moderate Mensheviks and Social Revolutionaries. One man, Alexander Kerensky, was a member of both the Provisional Government and the Executive Committee, and acted as a link between them.

▽ A meeting of the Petrograd Soviet in the Tauride Palace. As you can imagine, meetings were long and noisy, and decision-making not easy.

On 1 March the Soviet passed Order No.1:

> *The orders of the State Duma [that is, the Provisional Government] should be carried out only when they do not contradict the orders and decisions of the Soviet of Workers and Soldiers' Deputies [the full title of the Soviet]
> *All weapons must be under the control of soldiers' committees and must in no case be handed over to officers, even if they order it.
> *Addressing officers as 'Your Excellency', 'Your Honour' etc. is abolished and are replaced by 'Mr. General', 'Mr. Colonel' etc.

This makes it clear that the Petrograd Soviet had the real power. They not only controlled the use of armed force, but also the railways, the factories, even the electricity supply. However, having passed Order No. 1, they decided to let the Provisional Government get on with it, while keeping a critical eye on it to make sure that it recognised the concerns of workers and soldiers. Through March and April there were no serious disputes between the two bodies. There are several reasons for this:

- Everyone feared a tsarist counter-revolution. (In fact this fear ran throughout 1917, however unlikely it may appear to us – with hindsight.) The Soviet could see that the middle class liberals in the Provisional Government were more reassuring to the army commanders than the socialists in the Soviet.
- It was important to have some form of government to keep order.
- The Socialists knew their **Marxist theory** and decided that the February Revolution marked the beginning of the next, bourgeois, stage of history (and looking at the Provisional Government, they were quite right). They believed that this would last quite a while before the proletarian revolution would take place.

Look back to the diagram explaining **Marxism** on page 21.

What about the Bolsheviks?

The Bolsheviks were very much in a minority at this stage, in the Soviet and among workers and soldiers. Their leaders were abroad – Lenin had not been in Russia for ten years. **Stalin** and **Kamenev** did not return from exile until mid-March and then followed the orthodox Marxist line that Russia was entering the bourgeois stage of history, with the proletarian revolution a long way off. They even discussed co-operation with the Mensheviks and other socialist parties.

Stalin and Kamenev

Stalin was born in 1878 in Georgia; his real name was Joseph Djugashvili. He joined the Bolsheviks in 1903, was made Commissar for Nationalities in Lenin's government and became leader of the USSR after Lenin's death. Stalin died in 1953.

Kamenev was born in 1883 in Moscow and joined the Bolsheviks in 1902. He was deputy to Lenin from 1918 and was shot on Stalin's orders in 1936.

Lenin lights his historical beacon!

In exile in Switzerland, Lenin fretted to get back to Russia as soon as news of the February Revolution reached him, but his journey would mean having to cross German-held territory. Eventually the German government allowed him to travel to Russia via Finland and locked the doors of the train to prevent any possible contact with German Marxists.

As his sealed train rattled across war-torn Europe, he thought about the situation in Russia and jotted down his conclusions. Perhaps just because he was not there, not caught up in the daily events, his analysis was extraordinarily perceptive and led to a quite different plan of action for the Bolsheviks. It was like a beacon, illuminating four areas of the historical and political situation in Russia shown in the diagram below.

Lenin arrived at the Finland Station in Petrograd on 3 April. A leading Menshevik, Chkheidze, welcomed him but warned him that things were going fine and he shouldn't cause trouble. Lenin brushed him aside, climbed on to an armoured car and addressed the excited crowd. N.N. Sukhanov, a Menshevik who knew Lenin well, was there and remembered some of his speech:

'Dear Comrades, soldiers, sailors and workers! I am happy to greet in you the victorious Russian Revolution, and greet you as the vanguard of the worldwide proletarian army ... Long live the worldwide Socialist Revolution!'

Suddenly, before the eyes of all of us, completely swallowed up by the routine drudgery of the Revolution, there was presented a bright shining beacon.

▽ Lenin's conclusions on the historical and political situation in Russia, March/April 1917.

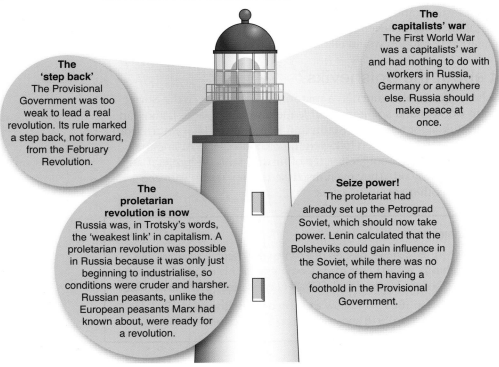

The 'step back'
The Provisional Government was too weak to lead a real revolution. Its rule marked a step back, not forward, from the February Revolution.

The capitalists' war
The First World War was a capitalists' war and had nothing to do with workers in Russia, Germany or anywhere else. Russia should make peace at once.

The proletarian revolution is now
Russia was, in Trotsky's words, the 'weakest link' in capitalism. A proletarian revolution was possible in Russia because it was only just beginning to industrialise, so conditions were cruder and harsher. Russian peasants, unlike the European peasants Marx had known about, were ready for a revolution.

Seize power!
The proletariat had already set up the Petrograd Soviet, which should now take power. Lenin calculated that the Bolsheviks could gain influence in the Soviet, while there was no chance of them having a foothold in the Provisional Government.

The April Theses

The next day Lenin set out his plans for the Bolsheviks, based on the notes he had made on his train journey across Europe. They were known as the April Theses:

- No co-operation with the Provisional Government.
- No co-operation with other parties.
- Organise for an immediate worldwide revolution.
- Call for a rapid end to the war.
- Call on the Soviets to take power in the name of the workers.
- Call for landowners' estates to be handed over to the peasants.

He expressed this programme in two powerful slogans:

'All Power to the Soviets!'

'Peace, Land and Bread!'

This programme destroyed the consensus which had existed since the February Revolution and set the Bolsheviks apart from everyone else. Of course, the impact was not felt at once. The leaders of other parties dismissed him as a 'has-been'. It took time for Lenin to win over his colleagues in the Bolshevik leadership (although, as we shall see, some rank and file members had reached the same position already). It took time for the swirling mass of people to hear about and take in what he proposed. But it meant that if ever they lost faith in other parties and the Provisional Government, they knew who to turn to.

Whether he was correct in his analysis, and therefore in his programme of action, would depend on the Provisional Government, and particularly how it dealt with the key issues Lenin had so sharply identified: 'Peace, Land and Bread'.

Was Lenin a German agent?

The fact that the German government arranged for Lenin to get into Russia, and had indeed given him money while he was in Switzerland, led to later charges from his enemies that he was a German agent. He certainly didn't take orders from Berlin, although he was happy to take their money in order to survive. For their part the German government calculated — correctly as it happened — that his presence in Russia would bring about a revolution and take Russia out of the war.

The Provisional Government's dilemmas

Peace!

The Provisional Government wanted to continue the war vigorously. They had taken on the treaty obligations made by the Tsar with Russia's allies, France and Britain. Further, Russia was bankrupt and needed the allies' financial backing if it was to survive. Several members of the Provisional Government, including Miliukov, wanted to fight on to gain territory for the Russian Empire, including seizing Constantinople (modern day Istanbul).

BUT most of the soldiers wanted only to fight a defensive war.

Matters came to a head on 5 May. It became known that Miliukov told the allies: *'Our business is to save Russia by ruthlessly prosecuting the war to victory'.* There were street demonstrations against him, and he was forced to resign. A new government was formed, which included the Menshevik Tsereteli and the Social Revolutionary leader Chernov, but it was still dominated by Kadets. Kerensky was made Minister of War.

Land!

The Provisional Government knew they had to deal with deep-rooted peasant demands for land. However, they feared that if land transfer to the peasants began, soldiers would desert and rush home to claim their share. Also, many duma members were property owners themselves; they wanted to ensure that land transfers were done legally and with compensation for landowners. The government therefore stalled, saying land reform could only be done by a properly elected Constituent Assembly.

BUT as 1917 went on, peasants increasingly took the law into their own hands and seized land – and there was nothing the government could do to stop them.

Bread!

The Provisional Government tried to deal with the food shortages which had been such a big factor behind the February Revolution by fixing the price of grain. They also announced a rationing system.

BUT the peasants wouldn't sell grain at the fixed price the government offered. The rationing system was still not in operation by the end of June and food shortages continued.

---

1 Look at Lifeline A (page 89) for the months from March to the middle of June.

   Do you agree with the pattern? If so, what evidence supports this pattern? If not, how would you draw the line? What evidence would you use to justify the shape of your graph?

2 Draw the first part of Lifeline B for the Provisional Government, up to the end of June.

   Is it a straight line? Does the gradient change at any point?

   Explain why you've given it that shape.

2: Mid-June–end of September: Kerensky's mistakes

By mid-June the window of opportunity to unite the country, which the Provisional Government had had since March, was rapidly closing.

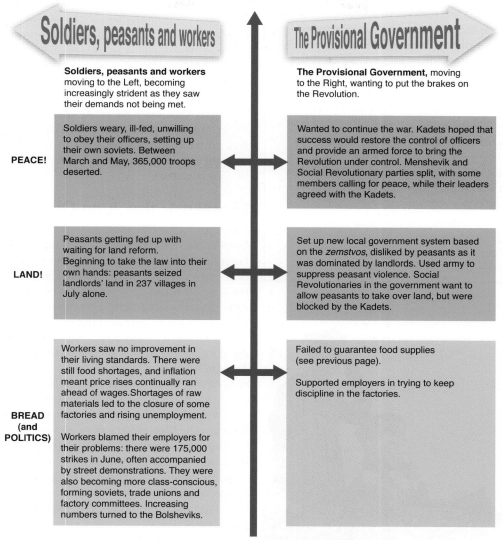

Soldiers, peasants and workers

Soldiers, peasants and workers moving to the Left, becoming increasingly strident as they saw their demands not being met.

The Provisional Government

The Provisional Government, moving to the Right, wanting to put the brakes on the Revolution.

PEACE!

Soldiers weary, ill-fed, unwilling to obey their officers, setting up their own soviets. Between March and May, 365,000 troops deserted.

Wanted to continue the war. Kadets hoped that success would restore the control of officers and provide an armed force to bring the Revolution under control. Menshevik and Social Revolutionary parties split, with some members calling for peace, while their leaders agreed with the Kadets.

LAND!

Peasants getting fed up with waiting for land reform. Beginning to take the law into their own hands: peasants seized landlords' land in 237 villages in July alone.

Set up new local government system based on the *zemstvos*, disliked by peasants as it was dominated by landlords. Used army to suppress peasant violence. Social Revolutionaries in the government want to allow peasants to take over land, but were blocked by the Kadets.

BREAD (and POLITICS)

Workers saw no improvement in their living standards. There were still food shortages, and inflation meant price rises continually ran ahead of wages. Shortages of raw materials led to the closure of some factories and rising unemployment.

Workers blamed their employers for their problems: there were 175,000 strikes in June, often accompanied by street demonstrations. They were also becoming more class-conscious, forming soviets, trade unions and factory committees. Increasing numbers turned to the Bolsheviks.

Failed to guarantee food supplies (see previous page).

Supported employers in trying to keep discipline in the factories.

A gap opened up between the Provisional Government and the workers, soldiers and peasants, which was widening by the day.

At the same time, the original supporters of the Provisional Government were losing faith in it.

- **Army officers** blamed the Provisional Government for their loss of command and the collapse of the Russian army as a fighting force.
- **Landowners** blamed it for being unable to stop peasants' attacks on their property.
- **Factory owners** blamed it for allowing the workers to form trade unions and restricting working to eight-hour days.

Kerensky

Alexander Kerensky was the most popular man in Russia in the summer of 1917.

- To workers and socialists he was a hero of the Left. He had run a socialist newspaper in the 1905 Revolution, been arrested afterwards and served four months in jail. He was not a Marxist, but belonged to the Trudoviks (see page 56). As a lawyer, he had given free legal advice to workers. He had been elected to the duma in 1912 and was a member of the Petrograd Soviet.

- To army commanders he stood for an aggressive continuation of the war. To the middle classes he was a bridge to the Soviet, a man who stood for law and order against revolutionary violence.

- He was a brilliant, dramatic speaker and self-publicist. He consciously modelled himself on Napoleon, who had won spectacular military victories for revolutionary France.

The Provisional Government always was a coalition of parties. As the difficulties increased, squabbles between different parties became more frequent and bitter. The eventual falling-out took place over the issue of national minorities' demands for independence. The Kadet members wanted to hold the great Russian Empire together. The socialist ministers were ready to make concessions to the Ukrainians. Fed up with the wrangling, Lvov resigned on 3 July, and Kerensky became Prime Minister.

Could Alexander Kerensky meet everyone's expectations and hold the country together? It was probably impossible anyway, but Kerensky brought about his own downfall by making two serious mistakes.

Mistake 1: the June Offensive

The reasons for continuing the war have already been explained – not wanting to lose territory to Germany, the need to stand by the alliances with Britain and France to ensure their financial backing, to shore up the position of the Provisional Government. Kerensky called for a new offensive in June and hurled himself into a frenzy of patriotic speeches. He emphasised the need for sacrifice; in a speech in the Bolshoi Theatre he said: *'I summon you to battle, to feats of heroism – I summon you not to festivity, but to death; to sacrifice yourselves for your country!'*

The middle class audience in the theatre loved the speech. The soldiers were less impressed.

The new offensive began on 16 June. It lasted three days before it turned into a rout. Thousands more soldiers lost their lives. Whole regiments deserted, some commandeering trains to take them home. This was surely predictable: the Provisional Government should have known that the state of the army, their weaponry and supply problems and especially their morale could only lead to defeat.

◁ This picture was widely circulated and shows Kerensky in military uniform, standing in the back of an open-topped car, reviewing Russian troops as Minister for War in May.

The July Days: a failed Bolshevik coup?

While the war was the government's priority all other reforms were on hold. Calling the **Constituent Assembly**, sorting out land reform and the food supply to the cities – all had had to wait.

The military disaster was now the cue for violent anti-government demonstrations from 3 to 6 July, known as the July Days. Angry workers were joined by soldiers from the Petrograd garrison and 20,000 armed sailors from the huge Kronstadt naval base nearby, who feared that they were being sent to the Front. Chernov, the Social Revolutionary leader, was nearly lynched by the sailors and only saved by Trotsky's cool head and quick thinking. Some of their frustration was recorded by N.N. Sukhanov, in the words of a worker who jumped on the platform of a Soviet Committee meeting and shouted:

> Comrades! How long must we workers put up with treachery? You're all here debating and making deals with the bourgeoisie and landlords. You are betraying the working class. Well, just understand that the working class won't put up with it! There are 30,000 of us here from Putilov. We're going to have our way! All power to the soviets! We have a firm grip on our rifles! Your Kerenskys and Tseretelis are not going to fool us!

Many in the government blamed the Bolsheviks for these demonstrations. Certainly, Bolshevik ideas and slogans were frequently heard on the streets during the July Days. Their support had been rising fast as frustration with the Provisional Government mounted. The accuracy of figures is open to doubt, but there were perhaps around 10,000 members of the Bolshevik Party in February and up to 75,000 members by July. But what did it mean to be a supporter or a member?

Support for different parties changed rapidly through 1917 as workers and soldiers swung behind whichever party seemed to express their ambitions most closely. Hardly anybody would have read Karl Marx, but many became increasingly aware of the Bolsheviks and the clear distinction Lenin had made between them and the other parties. Certainly, as the worker Sukhanov recorded above, they knew and liked Lenin's slogans. Members were more committed, attending meetings and (if they were literate) reading party newspapers and leaflets. Lenin wanted a disciplined, centrally-controlled Party, and indeed this is what the Communist Party later became. But as we shall see, there was a great deal of difference in 1917 between what he wanted and what the actual Party was like. The driving force behind the July Days seems to have come from grass-roots Bolsheviks ready to seize the moment.

Lenin was actually away from Petrograd when the July Days started, and returned only on 4 July. While not condemning the action, he refused to take a lead, judging that the time was not yet ripe. The rising petered out when troops loyal to the Provisional Government arrived.

> The expectation of almost everyone who supported the Revolution was that a democratically elected body, the **Constituent Assembly**, would decide on a new constitution for Russia.

Mistake 2: Kornilov

Kerensky took the opportunity of the failure of the July Days to strengthen his own position. Leading Bolsheviks were arrested. Lenin fled to Finland, accompanied by Provisional Government accusations of being a German agent. The Bolshevik newspaper *Pravda* was shut down. It was a low point for the Bolsheviks.

Kerensky formed a new government, composed of eight socialists (Mensheviks and Social Revolutionaries) and seven non-socialists, including four Kadets. This, the third coalition since February, might seem more radical than the first and second, but it was not. The Menshevik and Social Revolutionary members were from the right of their parties, and the four Kadet members exercised great influence. The moderate socialists were unwilling to push through their party policies against the Kadet members who had the support of factory owners and landlords. They didn't resign because they felt it was necessary to stay in the government for fear of a monarchist counter-revolution. However, in doing so they hopelessly weakened their parties' positions in the eyes of the people by being tainted with everything the Provisional Government did – or failed to do. Lenin described them as *'Those despicable socialists who have sold out'.*

The failure of the July Days and the suppression of the Bolsheviks led anti-revolutionary forces to flex their muscles. The Society for the Economic Rehabilitation of Russia, for example, dominated by the owner of the Putilov factory, pressed for an end to the 8-hour day, and the suppression of workers' factory committees. Then there was the Republican Centre, supported by bankers, industrialists and right-wing politicians. As their name suggests, they were not tsarists, but wanted a stable capitalist democracy. They made links with the Union of Landowners, who were resisting land transfer and demanding action against peasant violence.

The key, of course, was the army. On 18 July Kerensky appointed General Kornilov as Supreme Commander of the armed forces. As a typical army officer, he considered that his priority was to win the war. To do this, he made it clear that he needed to restore discipline in the army, which meant restoring court martials and the death penalty and breaking up soldiers' soviets. Regiments which had taken part in the July Days were disbanded and the **Kronstadt** garrison reduced. As for the socialists, he regarded them as the enemy within and made no bones about it: *'It's time to hang the German agents and spies, with Lenin at their head, and disperse the soviet so that it can never re-assemble.'* He was supported by the middle classes and the Kadets who saw him as their saviour against the revolutionaries.

In August the German army advanced further into Russian territory, closer to Petrograd. Refugees flooded into the city, adding to the atmosphere of panic. There were rumours of another attempted Bolshevik take-over.

What happened next between Kornilov and Kerensky is very confused, not helped by what they both said afterwards.

The changing situation is told on the opposite page.

Kronstadt

A huge naval base outside Petrograd. The sailors were mainly Bolshevik supporters (also see pages 116–117)

KORNILOV

Claimed that he had a 'pact' with Kerensky to move a strong, loyal force to Petrograd to crush left-wing parties, remove the Soviet and establish military control over armament industries.

August 27–29 he moves troops towards Petrograd.

Denounces Kerensky: *'I, General Kornilov, declare that under pressure from the Bolshevik majority in the Soviet the Provisional Government is acting in complete accord with the plans of the German General Staff… and is undermining the very foundations of our country.'*

Railway workers prevent Kornilov's troops from reaching Petrograd. He surrenders on 1 September.

KERENSKY

Said there was no such 'pact'. Kornilov's forces were simply needed to maintain order in the increasingly lawless Petrograd.

What is Kornilov really up to? Is he going to remove the Provisional Government and become military dictator? Kerensky changes his mind. He relieves Kornilov of his command: *'I order … General Kornilov to surrender the post of Supreme Commander … I call upon all ranks of the army and navy to their duty of defending the country.'*

Kerensky hands out weapons to workers (including many Bolsheviks released from prison) to defend Petrograd against Kornilov's troops.

Results of the Kornilov Affair

- Kerensky was totally discredited on all sides: army officers felt he had betrayed Kornilov and soldiers felt he had been part of an officers' plot to overturn all the gains made in the Revolution.
- Kadets were also discredited – they were now clearly seen to be supporters of industrialists and landowners.
- Mensheviks and Social Revolutionaries were discredited as associates of Kerensky and tainted by all the failures of the Provisional Government of which they were members.
- Bolsheviks gained support as the protectors of the Revolution.
- Many Bolshevik Party members and supporters formed armed companies, called 'Red Guards'.

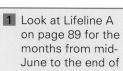

1 Look at Lifeline A on page 89 for the months from mid-June to the end of September.

Do you agree with the pattern drawn by the historian? If not, how would you draw the line?

How would you explain the shape of your chosen lifeline graph?

2 Draw the first part of Lifeline B of the Provisional Government, up to the end of September.

Is it a straight line? Does the gradient change at any point?

Explain why you've given it that shape.

3. October: Lenin seizes the moment

The Provisional Government: September to October

In early September the Bolsheviks gained a majority on the Petrograd city council and on 25 September Trotsky was elected Chairman of the Petrograd Soviet. At the same time Bolsheviks took control of the Moscow Soviet.

In late September Kerensky formed a new coalition government, still including non-socialist members. It was made up of obscure provincial SR politicians and a few Kadets, who nevertheless held all the key posts. It was the same mix as before and lasted just four weeks.

Fearful of the German army getting nearer to Petrograd, Kerensky ordered some of the city garrison to the Front. This provoked massive opposition and the Petrograd Soviet withdrew its support for the Provisional Government for the first time since March. Kerensky's authority was all but dwindling away. Meanwhile, queues for food in every city in Russia were getting longer and more desperate. Lawlessness was increasing, with gangs of deserters roaming the country. Travel was dangerous and looting common.

By then everyone expected the Bolsheviks to take power from the Provisional Government: it was just a question of when, and how.

■ As we get nearer to the actual events of the October Revolution, we need to go into greater depth about what we now know had been happening among the workers, soldiers and peasants during the events described on the last 14 pages. We are going to test the interpretations of Soviet and western historians in more detail against what we have learned from recent research.

To help you through this, here is a second activity. It will feed into the main activity with the two lifeline graphs which you began on page 89.

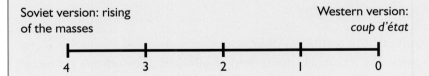

Soviet version: rising of the masses

Western version: coup d'état

```
├────────┼────────┼────────┼────────┤
4        3        2        1        0
```

Your task is to judge which of the interpretations is closer to what really happened, using the evidence on pages 103–112.

As you read through this section, place each of the key items – workers, soldiers, peasants – in a box on the line according to where you think the current evidence suggests they ought to go. Then we will consider Lenin's role slightly differently.

October – Soviet interpretations

By October the Bolsheviks had won the support of most of the population of Russia and Lenin played a key role in using this to take power.

- **Workers** in all industrial cities supported the Bolsheviks.
- **Soldiers** were coming round to the Bolsheviks.
- **Peasants**, especially poorer peasants, had been won over by the Bolshevik policy of re-distributing land to them.
- **Lenin played a leading role**: he gave undisputed leadership to the Bolsheviks through the whole October seizure of power.

October – western interpretations

Most ordinary Russians were naïve, poorly-educated, easily manipulated by Lenin and the Bolsheviks. Describing the soldiers and peasants, the British historian J.L.H. Keep writes of their *'total lack of political experience or understanding of what was happening …'* They were *'an easy prey to the agitators'* (1976).

- **Workers** were a tiny minority of the population; the Bolsheviks only had the support of workers in Petrograd, and that only briefly.
- **Soldiers'** support for the Bolsheviks was very patchy and short-lived.
- **Peasants** overwhelmingly stayed loyal to the Social Revolutionaries.
- **Lenin played a leading role;** he led the Central Committee of the Bolshevik Party, a tiny group of ruthless, power-hungry intellectuals, to seize power by armed force.

Getting up to date with recent interpretations

From the 1970s, historians both in Russia and the west began to reject both the interpretations described on the previous page as too narrowly concerned with top level politics. These new historians had a commitment to finding out about the lives of ordinary men and women. Their research into social history led to new angles on the politics, too. Many individual studies began to appear, of events in towns and cities outside Petrograd and Moscow, of parties other than the Bolsheviks and, particularly, of specific trades and factories. One example, the Petrograd laundresses' strike of May 1917, is described in the panel on the next page.

Research into grass-roots activity suggests that, as Steve Smith says on page 106, the Bolsheviks had become, by September *'… the only viable alternative'.* Membership of the Bolshevik Party grew by leaps and bounds through 1917, especially after the Kornilov Affair, with perhaps as many as 350,000 members by October. Most of these were worker activists. Far from doing what the Central Committee told them, they were more radical, always fearful of counter-revolution, calling for the immediate overthrow of the Provisional Government.

As you read this section, look for evidence that supports or challenges the interpretations on page 103.

Workers

Petrograd, with its population of 2.4 million, was the biggest city and the largest concentration of industry in Russia. During the war, the number of industrial workers in the city had risen by 60 per cent to nearly 400,000. Many of these new industrial workers were peasants, with little experience of factory, or urban life. An increasing proportion were women, forced to become breadwinners while their husbands were at war.

The Petrograd Laundresses' strike

This account is an example of the kind of research carried out by recent historians. It is only one strike, but gives grass-roots evidence of what was really going on.

On 1 May 1917 several thousand Petrograd laundresses went on strike. Their demands were: an eight-hour day, a minimum wage, proper pay-books showing hours worked and money earned, two weeks' notice to be given for sacking (rather than instant), better sanitary conditions in their laundries, a month's sick leave and more polite forms of address from their employers. To break the strike, employers hired non-union 'blackleg' workers and violence flared when the laundresses' union tried to extend the strike to other laundries. Other unions rallied round and their donations swelled a strike fund to pay the laundresses who were on strike. Mass meetings were held, some addressed by Alexandra Kollontai, the famous female Bolshevik. Gradually, employers had to give way, and by May 28 all the strikers' demands had been met.

The laundresses' strike is interesting for a number of reasons. It tells us about women's active role in the events of this momentous year, about the wide-ranging grievances the laundresses had, about the work of trade unions, and solidarity of workers from other industries. Also, importantly, it tells us about the Bolsheviks' readiness to show their support for workers in a dispute.

The laundresses' strike is typical of many industrial actions which took place in 1917. Their grievances are about what are usually called 'bread and butter' issues: wages, hours, working conditions, terms of employment, etc. It was these issues which had brought the workers out on to the streets in February, but their grievances did not disappear with the abdication of the Tsar. In fact, they got worse. The price of food continued to rise and wages continued to lag behind. Historians have calculated that 'real' wages (that is, what you can actually buy with the money in your pocket) fell by between 10 and 60 per cent, depending on your wages. Historians Diane Koenker and William Rosenberg have calculated that 92 per cent of strikes were solely to do with 'bread and butter' issues, rather than party political issues, as the graph opposite shows.

In response to their problems, a host of workers' organisations, all banned under the Tsar, sprang up after the February Revolution: trade unions, housing committees, workers' factory committees and – after August – Red Guard Committees. The demand for 'workers' control' of their factories did not mean that the workers actually ran the factory; rather, that they tried to work with management to solve problems. A Russian historian,

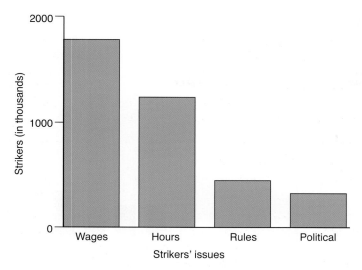

◁ Strikers' issues in 1917.

M.I. Itkin, has estimated that workers' committees were involved in the running of 74 per cent of Petrograd factories. In June and July, for example, many workers' committees were actively searching for raw materials to keep their factories open and operating. Times were desperate. A Bolshevik workers at the Putilov factory reported in June:

> The mass of workers in the factory are in a state of turmoil because of the low rates of pay, so that even we, members of the Workers Committee, have been seized by the collar, dragged into the workshop, and told 'Give us money!'

The time, commitment and persistence needed to participate in workers' committees over several months meant that members were increasingly the young, single – and more radical – workers. But the stresses of their situation were also pushing most workers towards more radical views. Bolshevik support for workers' outright control of factories meant that it was they who benefitted from this trend.

As the months went by, the gap between the parties in the Provisional Government and the workers' organisations began to widen. It was clear that the Kadets and their allies supported the factory owners in disputes. Analysis of newspapers shows that while Bolshevik papers reported strikes fully, Kadet papers either did not report them, or condemned them, arguing that strikes were an attack on the property of factory owners. Workers became disillusioned with other parties. A letter in 'The Worker' news sheet told readers:

> Because of profound misunderstanding I joined the Social Revolutionary Party, which has now passed to the side of the bourgeoisie and lent a hand to our exploiters … As a conscious proletarian, I am joining the Bolsheviks who alone are the defenders of an oppressed people.

The relative quiescence of workers in the early months of the Provisional Government, and their growing frustration in September and October can be seen in this chart of the numbers of strikes.

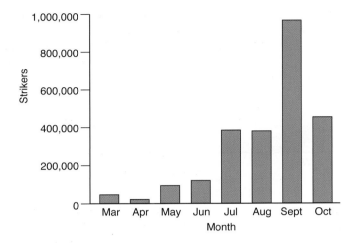

The number of ▷ people who took part in strikes all over Russia in 1917.

As it became clear that the Provisional Government was not going to deal with their problems, and following the Kornilov Affair, there was swelling support for the Bolsheviks in September and October. But this does not mean that workers were being 'manipulated' by the Bolsheviks. Thousands of workers were involved, in hundreds of soviets and committees of different kinds. Bolshevik organisation was tiny, by contrast. However, their propaganda put the workers' difficulties in the setting of their Marxist analysis of how capitalism works. As one worker wrote later:

> The Bolsheviks have always said 'It is not we who will persuade you, but life itself'. And now the Bolsheviks have triumphed because life has proved their tactics right.

British historian Steve Smith sums up what was happening:

> The workers had very concrete needs and expectations that the Provisional Government failed to meet. They turned to the Bolsheviks because their policies seemed to represent the only viable political alternative.

■ Where would you place **workers** on the line between Soviet and western historians' interpretations?

In factories all over Russia, workers supported Bolshevik-inspired resolutions and called for an all-socialist government to replace the Provisional Government coalition.

Soldiers

Soldiers had played an important role in the February Revolution, either actively as demonstrators or passively by refusing to crush civilian demonstrations. Sailors, too, were important; they were often more radical than soldiers, more of them being recruited from workers (particularly the more radical skilled workers), rather than from peasants.

Soldiers and sailors rapidly elected their own committees after February to deal with their grievances. These were mainly to do with the sheer brutality of their lives: harsh discipline and abusive officers. Some more sadistic officers were summarily dealt with, for example the admiral of the Baltic Fleet was thrown overboard to die in the icy waters. However, many officers joined their men, and new officers were elected. Christopher Read says:

> The takeover was spontaneous, orderly and responsible ... The need to maintain, rather than undermine, order was a key motive.

This democratisation process went on in all parts of the Front, in garrisons behind the lines, and in naval bases. In the early days, soldiers tended to support the Mensheviks and SRs. Out of about 700 elected representatives on the south west Front in May, only about 50 were Bolsheviks. The fact that many resolutions passed were about land transfer reveals the peasant origins of most of the soldiers. Most resolutions passed about the war were to continue fighting, but purely defensively.

As with the workers and peasants, disillusionment with the Provisional Government began slowly, but soon swept through the armed forces. Living conditions in the army remained terrible, with food supplies 60 per cent down from pre-war and medical supplies hard to come by. On the Western Front in June, for example, 181,000 soldiers fell ill, compared to 30,000 who had to be treated for wounds. These were intractable problems, but the Provisional Government seemed to make little headway in solving them. Russian soldiers were used to enduring hardship, but most were now demoralised and hungry, virtually living off the land. Kerensky's oratory failed to stir them up enough to make a success of the June Offensive. Then came the Kornilov Affair, and the Provisional Government's efforts to restore discipline, including shooting and corporal punishment. Fear of a counter-revolution led to rapid radicalisation of many soldiers' committees in September and October. Officers suspected of counter-revolutionary sympathies were arrested. Increasing numbers of soldiers began to fraternise with the Germans. The distinctive Bolshevik policy of calling for peace began to work in their favour. The Bolsheviks were alert to soldiers' other concerns too, promising to pay money to their wives and demobilise the over 40s. Many soldiers' committees now passed pro-Bolshevik resolutions and called for the Soviet to take power.

As you read this section, look for evidence that supports or challenges the interpretations on page 103.

Where would you place **soldiers** on the line between Soviet and western historians' interpretations?

As you read this section, look for evidence that supports or challenges the interpretations on page 103.

Peasants

The peasants had played little part in the February Revolution, but that did not mean that they were satisfied with their lot. Far from it! Their desire for a fairer division of land between themselves and their landlords was permanent and deeply felt. It was almost a religious belief, held by all, that land should belong to those who worked it. The rise in population from the late nineteenth century had made things worse and Stolypin's reforms (see pages 60–61) had made little difference.

The war had brought only further hardship. Half of all males in Russia had been conscripted by 1917. The majority of Russians (over 80 per cent) were peasants, so this hit peasant families hard, harder than industrial workers, many of whom were in protected occupations in war industries. 2.6 million horses had been commandeered for the army, removing the other main source of labour from the peasants, most of whom used a simple wooden one-horse plough.

The removal of tsarist government in February was the signal for peasants to begin their own revolution by taking over landlords' estates. Peasants in the province of Novgorod, for example, took over one of the Tsar's estates because those in charge had oppressed the peasants *'in unscrupulously fulfilling the orders of that traitor to the Russian people, Tsar Nicholas Romanov'*. So much for the 'Little Father'! Lenin took actions like this as support for his Party: *'Here was objective proof, proof not in words but in deeds, of the people coming over to the side of the Bolsheviks'*.

Unlike the industrial workers, who had to create their own organisations, such as trade unions and workers committees, the peasants already had theirs: the *mir*. The *mir* (the village council) was already by far the most important body in the lives of the peasants and it was through the *mir* and the *volost* (council for a small local area) that the peasants began to act. The intensity of land seizures seems to have been determined by the farming cycle: the most active months were March and September, just before the spring and autumn sowing. On the whole, these land transfers were carried out relatively peacefully. The historian John Channon sums up recent research on how this worked:

> There is clearly an emerging consensus among writers, western and Soviet, that the peasant movement was organised mainly by the peasants themselves, that it was … not wantonly destructive, nor characterised by bloodshed. Landlords usually received some land when it was parcelled out, although they were expected to work it themselves. If they could not manage, *'We will leave them to die like cockroaches in a trough'* as one peasant put it.

The peasants had always lived their lives removed from the commercial life of the nation. They were almost self-sufficient and didn't need the market nearly as much as the market needed them. Food production for the cities had fallen as the war continued, but this meant higher prices for what the peasants were prepared to sell. With few consumer goods available in the war years, peasants were even less prepared to produce more than they needed for their own consumption. The removal of the tsarist government officials, the land captains and police, meant that the peasants were virtually beyond the reaches of the state after February 1917.

The Provisional Government proved unable to deal with the situation to anyone's satisfaction. They had to get more food to the cities, but were unwilling to use force to coerce the peasants to sell more. They knew that the land problem had to be dealt with; indeed, land redistribution was a key policy of the Social Revolutionary Party, members of which were ministers in the Provisional Government, including Kerensky. On the other hand, their partners in the coalition, particularly the Kadets, had the support of landowners, and blocked SR attempts at land reform. Lenin scornfully characterised the Provisional Government's approach as:

Wait until the Constituent Assembly for the land; wait until the end of the war for the Constituent Assembly; wait until total victory for the end of the war.

The peasants were not prepared to wait and the gap between them and the Provisional Government widened. In July/August the Provisional Government sent in troops to stop peasant attacks on landlords' property on 39 occasions; in September/October troops were ordered in 105 times. Disillusionment with the Provisional Government grew. Bolshevik influence among the peasants was weak and, as we shall see, the SRs retained their overwhelming support. However, the Left SRs made big gains in support through the autumn. Their policies of immediate land transfer to the peasants, peace, workers' control of factories and an end to coalition government were indistinguishable from the Bolsheviks. By early October, Left SRs controlled their party in Petrograd and many other cities and army bases.

■ Where would you place **peasants** on the line between Soviet and western historians' interpretations?

Lenin's role

Both Soviet and western historians agree that Lenin played a leading role in the October Revolution. The only difference seems to be whether he was brilliant or wicked. In his three-volume *History of the Three Russian Revolutions,* published in Moscow in 1985–87, the Soviet historian P.A. Golub wrote about Lenin:

> He was able swiftly and precisely to evaluate the situation ... and to plan the most appropriate methods of struggle against the counter-revolution. And again, as at every sudden historical turning-point, the creative power of Lenin's genius was displayed.

Western historians point out that in his book *What is to be done?*, written back in 1902, Lenin explained the need to create a highly-centralised body of professional revolutionaries, ready to seize the moment when it came. October was his moment.

As you look at this dateline of the events of October, look for evidence of how important Lenin's role was.

■ As you read through the dateline, how important does Lenin seem to be? Start by choosing which of the four simple judgements below you agree with most nearly.

You could add to the simple statements, if you need to, and then explain your choice.

- Very important: he managed it all.
- Important: he was at the centre of events.
- Quite important: he was one of several key people.
- Unimportant: other people carried out the Revolution.

27 September	Lenin writes to the Central Committee of the Bolshevik Party from Finland. (There was still a warrant out for his arrest following the July Days, so he had to try to impose his will on the Central Committee by letter.) He urges them to seize power *'Otherwise the Bolsheviks will cover themselves with eternal shame and destroy themselves as a party ... History will not forgive us'*. However, other leading Bolsheviks were more cautious: Kamenev and Zinoviev wanted to wait, and Trotsky suggested waiting until the All-Russia Congress of Soviets (on which the Bolsheviks seemed likely to have a majority) on 20 October.
7 October	Lenin returns to Petrograd in disguise, calling for an immediate seizure of power.
10 October	The Central Committee of the Bolshevik Party meets in an all-night session. They agree with Lenin that the time is getting ripe to seize power, but no specific plans are made. Indeed, Kamenev and Zinoviev publish their view, to wait a bit, in a newspaper.
	Travel difficulties lead to the All-Russia Congress of Soviets, planned for 20 October, being postponed until 25 October. The Bolsheviks make use of the time gained and now begin to plan in earnest.
20 October	The Soviet sets up a Military Revolutionary Committee with three Bolshevik and two Left SR members. Trotsky is one of the three Bolsheviks; Lenin is not. All Petrograd garrison units are put under control of the MRC.

22 October	MRC puts Red Guard groups on armed readiness.
23 October	Garrison in the Peter & Paul Fortress declares support for the Bolsheviks.

The actions so far were very cautiously done. Lenin, Trotsky and the Bolshevik leaders seem uninformed about the strength of their support and many doubted whether, if it came to it, workers and soldiers would fight against government forces. Then Kerensky hands Lenin a gift: on the evening of the 23 October he shuts down two Bolshevik newspapers. Lenin portrays this rather puny action as the start of a counter-revolution.

24 October

Far from being confident, Lenin, Trotsky and the Bolsheviks are very nervous about their plans. There were so many uncertainties: would enough troops stay loyal to the Provisional Government to prevent the Bolshevik assault? Would the working people of Petrograd support them?

At dawn, under Trotsky's orders Red Guards take control of Petrograd's bridges and railway stations. They still fear that armed units loyal to the Provisional Government will try to storm the city. Kerensky, however, can find no one prepared to fight for him. It takes some time for the Bolsheviks to realise this, so that their capture of the city is virtually bloodless, but very slow.

25 October

All of Petrograd is now in the hands of the Bolsheviks except for the Winter Palace. At 11 a.m. Kerensky, Prime Minister of the Provisional Government, flees from Petrograd in a car 'borrowed' from outside the American embassy. This leaves the remainder of the Provisional Government in a room in the Winter Palace, defended by two companies of Cossacks, some young officer cadets and 200 members of the Women's Battalion.

In fact, the defending garrison not only has very little ammunition but almost no food. By the evening all except about 300 people have quietly disappeared. The Bolsheviks could have walked in.

However, they are delayed by their own problems. The assault on the Winter Palace has to be postponed several times by late arrivals and miscalculations. It should have taken place at 3 p.m., but the *Aurora* does not fire its blank shot until 9.40 p.m.. At once most of the remaining defenders of the Winter Palace flee, but not until nearly 2 a.m. on 26 October does a handful of Bolsheviks find the ministers and put them under arrest.

The American journalist John Reed described the scene which greeted him when he managed to slip into the Palace in the afternoon:

'At the end of the corridor was a large ornate room with gilded cornices and enormous crystal chandeliers ... on both sides of the parquet floor lay rows of dirty mattresses and blankets upon which occasional soldiers were stretched out. Everywhere was a litter of cigarette butts, bits of bread, cloths and empty bottles of expensive French wine.'

On 25 October the Military Revolutionary Committee had a proclamation:

To the Citizens of Russia!

The Provisional Government has been overthrown. State power has passed into the hands of the Petrograd Soviet of Workers and Soldiers Deputies Military Revolutionary Committee, which stands at the head of the Petrograd proletariat and garrison.

The cause for which the people have struggled – the immediate offer of a democratic peace, the abolition of landlord ownership of land, workers control over industry, the creation of a soviet government – this has been assured.

Long live the revolution of workers, soldiers and peasants!

The British historian Orlando Figes asks:

How many people took part in the insurrection? ... Trotsky himself claimed that 25,000 to 30,000 people 'at the most' were actively involved – about 5 per cent of all the workers and soldiers in the city. The few surviving pictures of the October Days ... depict a handful of Red Guards and sailors standing around on half-deserted streets. None of the familiar images of a people's revolution – crowds on the streets, barricades and fighting – are in evidence.

Life in Petrograd carried on as normal. Streetcars and taxis ran as usual; the Nevsky was full of the normal crowds and during the evening shops, restaurants, theatres and cinemas remained open... In the workers' districts things were just as quiet, judging by the police reports recently unearthed from the soviet archives. 'Everything was quiet on the streets' replied the Chief of the Okhtensk District. 'The streets were empty' added the Police Chief of the Spassky District.

Lenin's role

Look again at what Soviet historian P. A. Golub wrote about Lenin (on page 110). Having now read what happened in October 1917, was Lenin really 'a genius'?

It seems clear that:

- He didn't get all his own way.
- He was the driving force behind seizing power, but ...
- ... a new key figure, Trotsky, carried out the detailed organisation of how the city was to be taken over and the Provisional Government removed. (See pages 114–115 and 133 for more on Trotsky.)

■ Concluding your Enquiry

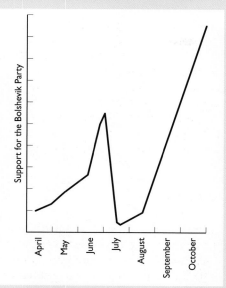

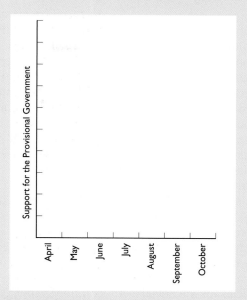

1 Look back over your responses to the activities you completed at the end of each of Sections 1 and 2. (Early March – mid-June: the window of opportunity and mid-June–end of September: Kerensky's mistakes).

   a) Did you agree with the suggested shape of Lifeline A? Does that suggest that the Bolsheviks were growing in popularity?

   b) Did your own Lifeline B, showing support for the Provisional Government, suggest that they were losing support by October?

2 Look back over your responses to the activities you completed at the end of each part of Section 3 (October: Lenin seizes the moment) using the interpretation line below. What were your decisions? Write a sentence explaining each of them:

   a) The level of Bolshevik support among workers (not just in Petrograd).

   b) The level of Bolshevik support among soldiers.

   c) The level of Bolshevik support among the peasants.

   d) The overall popularity of the Bolsheviks.

   e) The significance of the part played by Lenin.

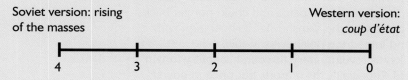

3 Which of the two interpretations: 'a rising of the masses', or 'a *coup d'état*', do you think comes closest to your own position?

   Or have you decided, like the revisionist historians, to reject the interpretations at both ends of the line? Can you write you own interpretation which fits closest to the history as we know it at present?

Trotsky (1879–1940)

Probably the most dynamic and talented of the leading Bolsheviks, Trotsky started life as Lev Bronstein, the son of a prosperous Jewish farmer in the Ukraine. The injustices of tsarist society, particularly the treatment of Jews, led him into revolutionary politics in his teens. He joined a group of Marxists and fell in love with one of them, Alexandra Sokolovskaya. They helped organise strikes, and he found real skill as a writer of revolutionary material, but they were caught by the *Okhrana*, imprisoned and exiled to Siberia in 1900. There, he married Alexandra and read widely in Marxist literature.

△ Trotsky in 1920.

In 1902, with Alexandra's help and taking the name of one of his guards, 'Trotsky', he escaped. He met Lenin in London and wrote articles for the Social Democrat newspaper, *Iskra* (The Spark). However, he could not agree with Lenin over his centralising tactics for the party. As he wrote much later:

> The party organisation takes the place of the party itself, the Central Committee takes the place of the party organisation, and finally the dictator takes the place of the Central Committee.

He was closer to the Mensheviks after the 1903 split with the Bolsheviks, (see page 44) although he did not join them, forming his own independent group. In Paris he met his second wife, Natalia Sedova, and stayed with her for the rest of his life, although he maintained good relations with Alexandra.

He came to the fore for the first time when the 1905 Revolution broke out, and was elected chairman of the St Petersburg Soviet. In Tsar Nicholas' counter-revolution he was arrested and put on trial, where his speeches revealed his power as a speaker. Imprisoned again, he escaped in 1907 and again fled abroad, living in Vienna, then Switzerland. He was in New York when the February 1917 Revolution took place and could not get back to Russia until May. He did not agree with the Mensheviks' co-operation with the Provisional Government and joined the Bolsheviks in July.

He brought to the Bolsheviks his revolutionary fervour, his ability to win support through his writing and, especially, his oratory, but once in power, he also demonstrated great skills of organisation. He was Chairman of the Petrograd Soviet, organiser of the October Revolution, then Commissar for Foreign Affairs in the Bolshevik *Sovnarkom* government (see page 119). Most essential of all, he inspired and organised the Communists' victory over all their opponents in the Civil War, living for most of two and a half years in his armoured train.

Trotsky was Lenin's obvious successor, but his brilliance, often arrogance, made him enemies. He was outmanoeuvred by Stalin, expelled from the Communist Party in 1928, from the USSR in 1929. He was assassinated in Mexico in 1940 on Stalin's orders.

The Russian revolutionaries saw themselves as creating a newer, better world, dealing with every aspect of people's lives. Some idea of this ambition, and of Trotsky's way of explaining them, can be read in these brief quotations from his many writings:

Marxism and worldwide revolution

The essence of Marxism consists in this, that it approaches society concretely, as a subject for objective research, and analyzes human history as one would a colossal laboratory record.
The completion of the socialist revolution within national limits is unthinkable.

Abolition of religion

The workers' state has rejected church ceremony, and informed its citizens that they have the right to be born, to marry, and to die without the mysterious gestures and exhortations of persons clad in cassocks, gowns, and other ecclesiastical vestments

Using the state to improve people's lives… or meddling in them?

There are two big facts which have set a new stamp on working class life. The one is the advent of the eight-hour working day; the other, the prohibition of the sale of vodka. Abusive language and swearing are a legacy of slavery, humiliation, and disrespect for human dignity, one's own and that of other people.

The state will take over all the tasks that were done in the home, so freeing the family, especially women

The workers' state must release the family from the burden of the kitchen and the laundry. Only under such conditions can we free the family from the functions and cares that now oppress and disintegrate it. Washing must be done by a public laundry, catering by a public restaurant, sewing by a public workshop. Children must be educated by good public teachers who have a real vocation for the work. The complete absorption of the housekeeping functions of the family by institutions of the socialist society, was to bring women, and thereby to the loving couple, a real liberation from the thousand-year-old fetters.

7 Was it the Civil War which turned the Bolshevik revolutionaries into Communist dictators?

In the dark early morning of 8 March 1921, almost exactly four years after the Revolution of February 1917, troops of the Red Army advanced towards their target. The Red Army was the armed force of the Bolshevik Party, (which had changed its name in June 1918 to the Communist Party). And who was their target? A tsarist general? Foreign invaders?

Not at all: they were being sent to crush the sailors, soldiers and workers of Kronstadt. Kronstadt is an island naval base twenty miles out from Petrograd and had provided some of the Bolsheviks' staunchest supporters in 1917. Their key role in the October Revolution led Trotsky to call them the *'pride and glory of the Russian Revolution'*. But the bitter disillusionment at Kronstadt four years later can be gained from this extract from their statement:

> **What we are fighting for:**
>
> By carrying out the October Revolution the working class had hoped to achieve its freedom. But the result has been an even greater enslavement of human beings. The power of the monarchy and its police … has passed into the hands of the Communist usurpers, who have given the people not freedom, but the constant fear of torture …
>
> They have laid their hands on the inner world of the toiling people, forcing them to think in the way that they want. Through the state control of trade unions they have chained the workers to their machines, so that labour is no longer a source of joy, but a new form of slavery. To the protests of the peasants, expressed in spontaneous uprisings, and those of the workers, whose living conditions have compelled them to strike, they have answered with mass executions and a bloodletting that exceeds even the tsarists. The Russia of the toilers, the first to raise the banner of liberation, is drenched in blood!

Their slogan: *'Soviets without Commissars!'* also tells us just how far their disillusionment with the Bolsheviks had gone.

The Communist leadership was determined to crush the mutiny. On 7 March they bombarded Kronstadt with heavy shells. The attack of 8 March took place in the open across the thick ice which, as long as it lasted, linked Kronstadt to the mainland. In a snowstorm, Red Army troops were mown down by the mutineers. A second, larger, assault, with 50,000 troops, was launched on 16 March, under the command of General Tukhachevsky, a tsarist general who had changed sides and risen to the top of the Red Army. Members of the Communist special police, the *Cheka*, stood behind their ranks with machine-guns, in case any of them tried to run away. 10,000 of them were killed in the attack. The Kronstadt mutineers fought house by house before the island was taken. Of the survivors, some escaped to Finland, but 500 were shot at once, 2000 more were executed later and hundreds sent to the first big Communist concentration camp.

■ Enquiry Focus: Was it the Civil War which turned the Bolshevik revolutionaries into Communist dictators?

Russia in 1921 was very different in many ways from what it was like in 1917.

- The only party permitted was the Communist Party. All other parties were banned.
- The Communist Party was centralised, controlled from the top, with no debate. It controlled all local and central government.
- Censorship was strict. Only Communist newspapers were published.
- The *Cheka* arrested, tortured and executed anyone suspected of opposition.
- Strict discipline was imposed in the Red Army.
- Factory workers had to do what they were ordered.
- Armed squads of *Cheka* went into the villages to seize the grain produced by the peasants.

What has happened to the idealistic Bolshevik revolutionaries of October 1917? Was it for this they had endured years of imprisonment and exile – to become vicious dictators?

Reaction to crisis

Some writers have described what Russia went through from 1918 to 1921 as being an equivalent crisis to the Black Death in fourteenth century Europe. There was a bitter civil war; the country was invaded by several foreign armies; large areas experienced a terrible famine; the transport system virtually collapsed; city-dwellers suffered years of near-starvation and the urban population fell by a third as people left for the countryside in search of food. Ten million Russians died.

In the years since the Revolution, people sympathetic to the Communists have pointed to this crisis to explain why they had created a dictatorial regime by 1921.

So here is your hypothesis to test in this chapter:

The Civil War forced the Communists to become dictators in order to ensure their own, and the Revolution's, survival.

As you read about what happened in Russia in the four momentous years after the October 1917 Revolution, you need to collect evidence which either supports this hypothesis or suggests a different one. The following dateline will help you keep the chronology under control.

October 1917:	Second All Russia Congress of Soviets meets. Council of People's Commissars *(Sovnarkom)* elected, with Lenin as head.
November 1917:	Bolsheviks take power in Moscow after 10 days of fighting. Coalition government of Bolsheviks and Left SRs formed. *Cheka* set up.
January 1918:	Constituent Assembly meets, and is closed.
March 1918:	Treaty of Brest-Litovsk signed with Germany. Left SRs leave coalition government in protest at Treaty terms.
March 1918:	Czech Legion begins to fight its way east.

Civil War Phase 1 begins (Reds v. mainly Greens)

June1918:	SR set up *Komuch* government in Samara.
July 1918	SR rising in Moscow. Tsar Nicholas and his family assassinated at Ekaterinburg.
August 1918:	Lenin shot by Fanya Kaplan.
Summer 1918:	By this time Estonia, Latvia, Lithuania, Finland, Poland, the Ukraine, Georgia, Armenia, Azerbaijan all declared independence.
November 1918:	Whites under Admiral Kolchak crush *Komuch* Republic.

Civil War Phase 2 begins (Reds v. mainly Whites)

January 1919:	Polish army invades the Ukraine.
October 1918:	Denikin's White Army gets within 200 miles of Moscow. Yudenich's White Army reaches suburbs of Petrograd.
January 1920:	Kolchak captured by Reds. Yudenich arrested by Reds.
April 1920:	Denikin's White Army defeated by Reds, Denikin escapes. Polish invasion of Russia.
August 1920:	Tambov region under peasant control.

Civil War Phase 3 begins (Reds v. Greens, peasant armies and armed bands)

March 1921:	Kronstadt mutiny crushed.
October 1921:	Famine in the Volga region. Peace treaty with Poland. Tambov rising crushed. Civil War peters out.

Reds	= Bolsheviks
Greens	= Non-Bolshevik socialists (mainly SRs and Mensheviks)
Whites	= Mainly Tsarists

The growth of Bolshevik dictatorship

Lenin remarked to Trotsky, in the small hours of 26 October, *'from being on the run to supreme power makes one dizzy'*. As you have seen, the Bolshevik seizure of power on 25 October 1917 had been remarkably easy. But their position was precarious and many observers said they would not last more than three weeks.

The new government was called The Council of People's Commissars, or *Sovnarkom* (Commissar meant Minister), with Lenin as Chief Minister. All the first Commissars were Bolsheviks, and their meetings were still much more like a revolutionary conspiracy than the government of a major power. Officials often refused Commissars entry to the ministry they were supposed to be in charge of. Officials at the State Bank refused to give them control of the country's finances until Red Guards went in and forced the clerks to hand over five million roubles, which they took away in a velvet bag and dumped on Lenin's desk.

The Bolsheviks had put years into plotting how to seize power but had almost no plans for what to do once they had it. They were amazingly naïve, falling back on simplistic Marxist utopianism: as late as September 1917 Lenin had said:

> Power to the Soviets means the complete transfer of the country's administration and economic control into the hands of the workers and peasants, to whom nobody would offer resistance and who, through their own experience, will soon learn how to distribute land, products and grain properly. [*They genuinely expected money to become unnecessary as]* under Communism products are not exchanged for one another; they are not bought and sold. They are simply stored in the communal warehouse and delivered to those who need them.
>
> (*ABC of Communism*)

It would be worth going over Marx's ideas again, using the diagram on page 21.

On the other hand, they were pragmatic, used to dealing with events as they occurred, giving orders 'on the hoof', as we shall see.

The Second Congress of Soviets

Just as the *Aurora* fired its guns as the signal for the assault on the Winter Palace, late in the evening of 25 October, the Second All-Russia Congress of Soviets opened. In a packed room, its atmosphere thick with smoke, socialists from all over Russia were gathered. About 300 of the 670 delegates were Bolsheviks, with 193 SRs, about half of whom were Left SRs, and 82 Mensheviks. Hardly had the Congress started when the Mensheviks and SRs bitterly denounced the Bolshevik removal of the Provisional Government as a 'criminal venture' and walked out. This played into the Bolsheviks hands. Trotsky famously denounced them: *'Your role is played out! Go where you ought to go – to the dustbin of history!'* Only the Bolshevik majority, and a minority of Left SRs, were left behind to cheer Lenin's Manifesto 'To all Workers, Soldiers and Peasants', proclaiming 'Soviet Power'.

Mensheviks and **SRs** also held Marxist views – see page 41 for details of these parties.

This does not sound like a party willing to work with others, does it? Only a few hours after the October Revolution a leading Bolshevik is pleased to see rival socialists relegated to 'the dustbin of history'. Are these early signs of one-party dictatorship?

However, outside the Congress it was quite clear that soviets, workers and soldiers expected to see a broad coalition of socialist parties. Under pressure from the Railwaymen's Union, Lenin was forced to include Left SR Commissars in *Sovnarkom*.

Class enemies

Before 1917 was over, the Bolsheviks began to attack those they saw as enemies. First, all newspapers of centre or rightist opinions were shut down; the Kadet Party was banned; leading Mensheviks and Right SRs were arrested. Workers were encouraged to attack 'class enemies' – especially the middle classes. The term for 'bourgeois' in Russian (*burzhoois*), came to mean not just bankers, factory-owners and merchants, but landowners, priests, speculators. In fact anyone well-dressed was likely to be abused, even assaulted, in the street.

Lenin

▽ Lenin in 1917.

The Bolshevik Party liked to be called 'a party of a new type'. It existed to overthrow capitalism and bring about the highest stage of human existence – communism. That meant that the leadership was not there to implement resolutions passed by its members. They despised that approach as 'tailism' – meaning that the leaders would be merely the tail of the dog, wagging to order. The Bolshevik leadership believed that only they, as revolutionary Marxist intellectuals, fully understood the best interests of the proletariat. They were therefore not the servants of the members, but their teachers.

Other parties were a threat and a distraction from the real task of building the communist future.

As a Marxist party, the Bolsheviks believed in class conflict. Certain people – the bourgeoisie – were class enemies. To the Bolsheviks, class enemies were not just to be ignored, but eliminated.

Added to that was Lenin. You have read enough about him already to know that he was a very forceful, determined character. He was difficult to work with, even for members of his own party: the chances of Lenin working in a coalition with other political leaders was slim.

■ The Civil War has not started yet and already an alternative hypothesis is beginning to emerge: that Lenin and the Bolsheviks wanted to set up a one-party dictatorship. Subsequent critics of the Communists say that dictatorship was built in from the start.

Here are the seven features of Communist dictatorship listed at the beginning of this chapter.

- The only party permitted was the Communist Party. All other parties were banned.
- The Communist Party was centralised, controlled from the top, with no debate. It controlled all local and central government.

- Censorship was strict. Only Communist newspapers were published.
- The *Cheka* arrested, tortured and executed anyone suspected of opposition.
- Strict discipline was imposed in the Red Army.
- Factory workers had to do what they were ordered.
- Armed squads of *Cheka* went into the villages to seize the grain produced by the peasants.

Which of these features can you find evidence of in what you've read already? Make notes on these early signs of dictatorship under the heading **Lenin and Bolshevik dictatorship**.

First Decrees of the Bolshevik government

In their first few weeks, the Bolshevik government passed a series of decrees.

- ■ Peasants had the right to take over landlords' estates without compensation and decide for themselves how to divide it up. Land now belonged to the people: it could not be bought, sold or rented.
- ■ Workers' committees had the right to control factories.
- ■ Old age pensions, sickness and unemployment benefits introduced.
- ■ National minorities had the right to decide if they wanted to become independent. (As the Bolsheviks did not control any of the national minority areas this decree existed on paper only.)
- ■ To end the First World War immediately. (This was, of course, totally ignored by all the fighting nations.)
- ■ Abolition of all titles and class distinctions. Everyone was now simply called *tovarich* (comrade).
- ■ Equality for women.
- ■ The government took over all banks, transport and industry. The Supreme Council of State Economy, *Vesenkha*, was set up to run them.
- ■ Private trade and businesses were banned.
- ■ All foreign debts were cancelled without compensation.

These first two decrees were not as important as they look: these things were happening anyway, but the decrees gave legitimacy to peasant and worker actions. Peasant land seizures certainly increased and both decrees gained popularity for the new government.

The *Cheka*

The Extraordinary Commission for Combating Counter-Revolution and Sabotage, or *Cheka*, was set up in December 1917. Led by Felix Dzerzhinsky, it became the main instrument of Bolshevik terror. By mid-1918 it had 1000 members, and was based in the **Lubianka**, a name which became synonymous with terror throughout the Soviet era. A founder-member explained: *'The Cheka is not an investigating committee, or a court... it is a fighting organ ... It does not judge, it strikes.'* Between 1918 and 1921 the *Cheka* put many thousands of Russians to death. But that was not the point: the main point was the terrorising of the rest of the population.

■ Note the date of setting up the *Cheka*: are the Bolsheviks building an organisation to terrorise those fellow-citizens they do not like?

Lubianka
This was the building which housed the headquarters of the *Cheka* (and later the KGB) and the associated prison

Constituent Assembly

An elected assembly had been the goal of every democratic protest movement in Russia for decades, from the Kadets to the SRs. In many towns and cities the Bolshevik Revolution had been accepted in the expectation that it was temporary, until the Constituent Assembly had met. In Saratov, for example, the Soviet took power and declared that 'its decisions were binding until resolution by the Constituent Assembly'.

The Provisional Government had been criticised for not getting on with the elections, but organising Russia's first democratic election was a huge undertaking. With universal franchise for all men and women over the age of twenty, the electorate was the biggest in the world, with potentially 80 million voters, most of whom were illiterate. Lenin did not dare to cancel the elections. They were held in November; about 40 million people voted.

The Bolsheviks won the support of workers in Petrograd and Moscow, among soldiers in the garrisons at home and, to a lesser extent, soldiers at the Front. They were overwhelmed by a tidal wave of peasant votes for the SRs, but this did not worry them. They represented the **proletariat**, so now they believed they had the right to take power – alone.

Remember that the **proletariat** was the industrial working class identified by Karl Marx as the force behind the overthrow of Capitalism (see page 21).

Party	Millions of votes	Percentage of votes cast
SRs	21.8	53
Bolsheviks	10.0	24
Kadets	2.1	5
Mensheviks	1.4	3
Others	6.3	15

▷ Election results in Russia, November 1917.

The next time Russians had a free democratic vote was in 1989.

The Assembly met on 5 January 1918 – and was closed down the next day by Bolshevik Red Guards, acting on Lenin's orders.

It was a momentous act. From then on, any hopes for multi-party democracy in Russia were dashed and a crucial step had been taken on the road to Civil War. What options did other socialist parties have, except armed opposition?

■ What do these events suggest about the hypothesis that **The Civil War forced the Communists to become dictators in order to ensure their own, and the Revolution's, survival**?

Under the heading, **Lenin and Bolshevik dictatorship**, make notes on:

a) The *Cheka*.

b) The Bolsheviks' treatment of the Constituent Assembly.

Making peace

From right back in the **April Theses** the Bolsheviks had promised to end the war. But when it came to it, they were split. Lenin wanted immediate peace with Germany. Even if the terms were harsh, he believed that the world-wide revolution which Marx had prophesied was about to happen, so any treaty would be nullified very soon. Others, led by **Bukharin**, wanted to continue the war as a revolutionary war, spreading Bolshevism into Germany and beyond, as in the French Revolutionary wars. Trotsky proposed 'neither peace nor war', but to open peace talks, so the fighting stopped, and keep them going as long as possible, spreading propaganda and waiting for the revolution to take Germany out of the war.

Peace negotiations began in December 1917, and reopened in the new year with Trotsky treating the German leaders to long political speeches. By early February the German High Command had lost patience. They signed a separate peace with Ukrainian nationalists, taking them out of the war, and reopened their invasion of Russia. They advanced 150 miles in five days, threatening Petrograd itself. This removed all the Bolsheviks' options and on 3 March they were forced to sign the Treaty of Brest Litovsk.

April Theses
Lenin's call on his return to Russia in April 1917, for 'Peace, Land and Bread' (see page 95)

Bukharin
(1888–1938) Bolshevik and member of Politburo

◁ The terms of the Treaty of Brest Litovsk.

It was probably the most ferocious peace treaty of modern times. Russia lost Poland, Finland, Lithuania, Latvia, Estonia, the Ukraine, Georgia and Belorus. These territorial losses included 60 million people (one-sixth of the population), 32 per cent of the Russian Empire's farmland, 54 per cent of its industry, 89 per cent of its coal mines and 26 per cent of its railway system. In addition, they had to pay Germany three million roubles 'reparations'.

Russians on the Right and the Left were absolutely horrified at what had been done to their country. In agreeing to the Treaty, Lenin had isolated the Bolsheviks. The Left SRs refused to have any more to do with the *Sovnarkom* government. Their armed rising marks the beginning of the Civil War. They assassinated the German ambassador and nearly killed Lenin who was shot, twice, by Socialist Revolutionary Fanya Kaplan.

Roman Stashkov becomes a diplomat

The Bolsheviks were keen to show the German High Command that they were dealing with a revolutionary democracy. Their delegation to the peace talks at Brest Litovsk was therefore supposed to include ordinary soldiers, sailors, workers, women and peasants. At the last moment, on the way to the station, they realised that they hadn't got a peasant with them. (This in itself tells you something about the Bolsheviks!)

Just then they spotted an old man with a long beard and peasant coat. He was a peasant called Roman Stashkov, on his way to a different station to catch a train back to his home in central Russia. Having established that he supported the Left SRs, they offered Roman a lift, but he became disturbed when he realised they were heading for the wrong station. He calmed down, however, when they promised to pay him.

At Brest-Litovsk his table manners at diplomatic banquets caused some comments from the aristocratic Germans, but Roman soon got over not knowing how to use a knife and fork and enjoyed the plentiful food. Asked whether he wanted red or white wine, he asked the German sitting next to him, Prinz Ernst von Hohenloe, 'Which is the stronger?'

And so Roman Stashkov entered diplomatic history as 'the plenipotentiary representative of the Russian peasantry'.

The Civil War

The next four pages help you to understand the pattern of events, but do not involve work on the Enquiry; we'll come back to that on page 128.

Whatever the problems already facing the Bolsheviks, the real crisis began with the Civil War.

The Civil War was a complex, confused affair – it has been estimated that there were 23 separate armies on Russian soil in 1919. It is the job of the textbook writer to present some patterns to help the reader through the confusion. Previous textbooks have chosen to present the war as a two-sided conflict: Reds (Bolsheviks) versus Whites (mainly tsarists). Unfortunately that simple view will no longer do. For one thing, it is a Bolshevik view of their opponents, labelling them all the same, when in fact there were huge differences between those who fought against the Communists. For another, it is a Petrograd/Moscow view of the war when important events were taking place far away from the two great cities.

We have already seen that historians researching new topics and new areas in recent years have come up with new insights. Research into what was going on in the vast expanses of the violently disintegrating Russian Empire has changed our view of the Civil War. A different pattern is now evident, based on three chronological phases:

1. June–November 1918: mainly Reds versus Greens.
2. November 1918–Autumn 1920: Reds versus mainly Whites.
3. Summer 1920–end of 1921: Reds versus mainly Greens and peasant armies and armed bands.

> Reds: Bolsheviks
>
> Greens: non-Bolshevik socialists (mainly SRs and Mensheviks)
>
> Whites: mainly tsarists

Phase 1 June–November 1918: Reds versus Greens

The SRs felt they had been driven into armed opposition. They had been outflanked and then ridiculed by Trotsky at the Second Congress of Soviets in October 1917. Their clear mandate to rule given in the Constituent Assembly elections had been stolen from them. The Left SRs in the *Sovnarkom* government walked out over the terms of the Treaty of Brest Litovsk. Then an unexpected opportunity occurred in the city of Samara, 500 miles east of Moscow.

During the First World War, Czech nationalists had formed their own volunteer army to fight alongside Russia to win independence from their Austro–Hungarian rulers. This Czech legion of 40,000 men now found themselves cut off from their homes by the boundary changes made by the Treaty of Brest Litovsk. In May 1918 they decided to use the Trans-Siberian Railway to travel to the Far East and get home that way. They were well-armed and took possession of several towns along the railway, including Samara. Local SR leaders negotiated with the Czechs to set up a government under their protection, and the Czech legion soon drove out the small local Red force.

The SRs called their government the Committee of Members of the Constituent Assembly (*Komuch*) and saw themselves as a government of patriotic socialists, the legitimate government of Russia, in exile. They controlled an area of several thousand square kilometres in western Siberia, where they carried out what an SR national government would have done: peasant land reform, encouragement of workers' participation in running factories through trade unions, state control of the economy. SRs in the north near Archangel also took power there for a while, but it was difficult to combine the two risings.

In the end it was not the Bolsheviks but the Whites who put an end to the Samara government. When the First World War ended in November the Czechs headed for home via the far east and the USA. A White army under Admiral Kolchak took over and arrested the *Komuch* ministers.

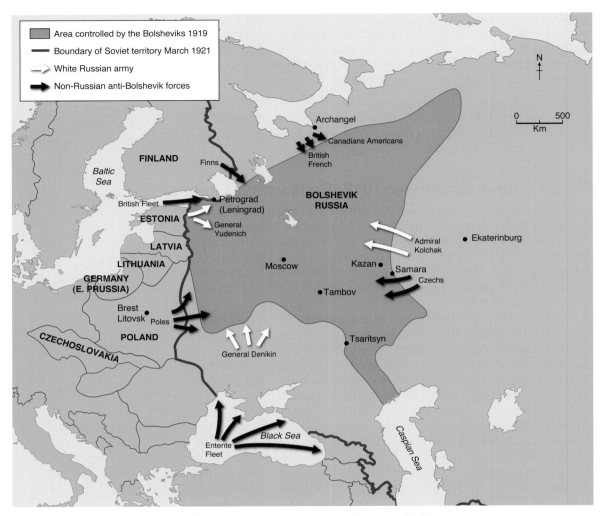

Key:
- Area controlled by the Bolsheviks 1919
- Boundary of Soviet territory March 1921
- White Russian army
- Non-Russian anti-Bolshevik forces

N

0 — 500
Km

Baltic Sea

FINLAND

Finns

Archangel
Canadians Americans
British
French

BOLSHEVIK
RUSSIA

British Fleet
Petrograd
(Leningrad)

ESTONIA
General
Yudenich

LATVIA

LITHUANIA

GERMANY
(E. PRUSSIA)

Brest
Litovsk
Poles

CZECHOSLOVAKIA

POLAND

Moscow

Tambov

Tsaritsyn

General Denikin

Ekaterinburg

Admiral
Kolchak

Kazan

Samara
Czechs

Entente
Fleet

Black Sea

Caspian Sea

△ The map shows the main areas of conflict, and reveals quite dramatically the weakness and, as we shall see, the strength of the Bolshevik position; at one stage they held no more than one-sixth of the country.

Phase 2 November 1918–Autumn 1920: Reds versus Whites

A number of right-wing armies, the Whites, threatened the Bolsheviks in the longest phase of the Civil War.

■ **Admiral Kolchak** led a tsarist army in the east from November 1918 and set up a right-wing government in Omsk, ruling a large part of western Siberia. Eventually he was forced to retreat through 1919 before being captured and shot by the Reds in 1920.

- **General Denikin** had been Kornilov's Chief of Staff and took over a large tsarist army in the south when Kornilov was killed in April 1918. He had the support of the Cossacks of the Don area and Kadet leaders. Having advanced northwards, his forces nearly succeeded in joining up with Kolchak's at Tsaritsyn by the summer of 1918. Tsaritsyn was just held by the Red Army under Stalin and the city was later renamed Stalingrad. In 1919 Denikin got to within 200 miles of Moscow but was forced to retreat right back to the Crimea. His forces were eventually evacuated by British and French naval vessels in 1920.
- **General Yudenich**, another ex-tsarist general, advanced through Estonia and reached the outskirts of Petrograd in October 1919 before being forced back.

Foreign armies

Other nations supplied the anti-Bolshevik forces with money and arms, and in some cases sent troops. Winston Churchill was determinedly anti-Bolshevik and at his instigation British forces were sent to Murmansk. French investors were the biggest losers when the Bolsheviks nationalised foreign businesses without compensation and the French fleet was sent to the Black Sea. Japanese forces occupied Vladivostok, hoping to seize territory; US forces were sent to keep an eye on the Japanese. On the whole there was little support at home for these expeditions. The foreign armies had little effect on the outcome of the Civil War. All had withdrawn by 1920.

> Foreign armies were mostly made up of working class men from Britain, France and Japan. They often sympathised with the Bolsheviks and were not keen on a war against a workers' republic.

The Polish War, 1919–21

In 1919 there were national and religious uprisings in central Asia and the Caucasus. However, the most serious threat came from newly independent Poland. The Polish army was successful at first. They **invaded** and reached Kiev, but were driven back to Warsaw by the Red Army under General Tukhachevsky. The Reds, however, could not sustain this advance and were driven out of Poland. Peace was made at the Treaty of Riga, 1921, at which Poland made significant gains of former Russian land in the Ukraine and Belorus.

> The **invasion** of Russia by the Poles and fierce fighting which following embittered Russian-Polish relations for a generation.

Phase 3 August 1920–end of 1921: Reds versus Greens (and others)

A third phase of Civil War broke out in late summer 1920. Although the Whites were defeated, the Red Army was fully stretched against the Poles and resistance to the Communists was widespread: there were plenty of grievances against the Communists by then, from harsh discipline in the factories, hunger in the cities and forced grain requisitions in the countryside (see War Communism, below). However, the SRs were so weakened by this time that they could not launch the co-ordinated effort needed to oust the Communists.

In August, peasants in a village in the Tambov region, 200 miles south east of Moscow, attacked a Red grain requisition brigade and killed several of them. They were joined by other villagers and by the end of the year 8000 brigade members had been killed. Although some local and former SRs took a leading role, these were peasant risings. They had no intention of taking over the government, but effectively cut the whole province off from Communist control for over a year. Similar peasant risings (too numerous, and too local to list) took place all over Russia. These peasant bands used **guerrilla warfare**, such as blowing up bridges, cutting telegraph lines and pulling up railway tracks, to defeat all attempts by the Communist government to bring them into line. They used terror of their own, mutilating the bodies of those they captured in a savage war of vengeance.

The peasants of Tambov were only crushed when a huge Red Army of 100,000 men moved into the province in the last part of 1921.

We should also add to this phase of the Civil War the bitter strikes in Moscow in the summer of 1920, the appearance of a group called the Workers' Opposition within the Bolshevik Party, and, of course, the Kronstadt mutiny of March 1921 (see page 116).

Makhno

Nestor Makhno (1889–1934) was a Ukrainian peasant leader and **anarchist**. He believed that free peasants and peasant soviets should run their own affairs with no central government control. A brilliant guerrilla leader, he mobilised an unbeatable force of 15,000 partisans, including cavalry, and became a local hero in the Ukraine. He fought the Germans and the Whites and then, as the Bolsheviks turned against him, he fought the Reds too. On the run by August 1921, he fled to Romania. From there he moved to Paris, where he worked as a carpenter and stage-hand at the Paris Opera, at film studios, and at the Renault factory.

War Communism

By mid-1918 the Bolsheviks were fighting for their very existence. War Communism is the name given to the set of drastic measures taken by Lenin and the Bolsheviks to win the Civil War and stay in power.

War Communism in industry

By 1918 industrial production was running at about 30 per cent of 1913 levels. The problems faced by the Provisional Government in 1917 – lack of raw materials, failures of the transport system, inflation – had only got worse. Management of factories by workers' committees was not working. The flight of workers from the cities to the villages was causing a labour shortage.

All industries had been put under centralised state control in December 1917 and were now run by the Supreme Council of State Economy, *Vesenkha* (see page 121). The *Vesenkha* solution was to bring discipline to the factories. Workers were fined for lateness, or not meeting their output target. Each worker was issued with a record-book, without which they could not get their food rations. Trade unions were taken over by Communist Party officials, who were appointed, not elected, and used the unions to give orders to the workforce. Managers and experts who had been sacked in the Revolution for being members of the bourgeoisie were brought back to make the factories, especially the arms factories, run again.

War Communism and the peasants

To win their support for the Revolution, Lenin had agreed to support the peasants' demand for land. But the Bolsheviks were never a peasant party and were suspicious of what they saw as 'bourgeois values' among the peasants. Further, the food problem in the cities, a major cause of the February Revolution, was reaching a serious crisis. In Petrograd, the daily food ration for all non-workers (including children) in mid-1918 was 50 grams – one slice of bread. The loss of the Ukraine, a major grain-producing area, at the Treaty of Brest Litovsk made matters worse. Industrial goods were so scarce, and at such high prices, that the peasants saw no point in sending food to market. They had virtually fallen back to being subsistence farmers.

However, the Bolsheviks were convinced that the peasants were deliberately hoarding food. Armed *Cheka* units were sent into the countryside to seize grain. Grain requisitioning squads of 75 men with two machine-guns overcame peasant resistance. Sometimes they took everything, even the seed-corn for the next year. Lenin's instructions were often ruthless: *'Hang no fewer than a hundred well-known rich bags and blood-suckers and make sure the hanging takes place in full view of the people'.* It was a Bolshevik war on the peasants. The peasants responded with passive resistance: the area of land sown fell by 17 per cent in 1919 and another 11 per cent in 1920.

War Communism: terror and the *Cheka*

Tsar Nicholas, the Tsarina Alexandra and their children had been placed under house arrest at Ekaterinburg, well away from big cities. On 17 July 1918 local Bolsheviks ordered them into the cellar of the house and machine-gunned them all. Their bodies were then covered with acid and thrown down a mine-shaft.

They were just the most famous of the victims of the growing Bolshevik terror. The Civil War, the assassination attempt on Lenin, the growing opposition to the Bolsheviks among disgruntled workers, peasant resistance to the grain requisitioning squads, all led to an increase in the power and influence of the *Cheka*. Prisoners were executed without trial. Torture was common. By the end of 1918 there had been 6300 official executions, but this figure is possibly the tip of the iceberg. One historian, Robert Conquest, has estimated the number of deaths at the hands of the *Cheka* at 500,000 by 1921. The *Cheka* itself had become a distinct élite, living separately in their own compounds, with their own well-stocked shops, restaurants and sports facilities. They were said to specialise in recruiting orphans, so that their members were totally dependent on the *Cheka* as their only family.

Russia in 1921: the depths of disaster

By 1921 the Reds had won the Civil War but ruled a country in the depths of disaster.

Accurate figures are impossible to establish, but probably ten million Russians died between 1917 and 1921. At least five million died in a famine which hit the Volga region. This was caused partly by crop failure, but also by the grain requisitioning squads who left the peasants no grain to plant, and by the disruption of agriculture caused by the Civil War.

Another million died of diseases such as typhus and influenza, which ravaged a population weakened by lack of food and medical care.

In the cities

Workers had to spend three-quarters of their wages on food. Rations were so short that enough food could only be obtained through the black market. Cuts in food rations in January 1921 led to demonstrations which were broken up by the *Cheka*. So many people had fled the cities for the villages that the population of Petrograd, for example, had shrunk from 2.5 million in 1917 to 0.75 million by 1921. Water and electricity were rarely available.

Members of the 'former classes', as the middle classes were called, were hardest hit. Two million had emigrated. Rations were calculated on a class basis, so a worker got more than a bourgeois. Housing was controlled by committees, so that the former owners of a large house could find themselves living in one room, sharing their former home with several families. Many members of the 'former classes' were compelled to do labouring work (see photo 2 on page 17).

In the countryside

The Bolsheviks had almost lost control. Less and less food reached the cities. Peasant rebellions were increasing.

The railways hardly functioned, blocked by abandoned trains which were home to gangs of bandits, or filled with the bodies of typhus victims.

▽ This photograph from 1921 shows children in the Volga region suffering from severe malnutrition.

The Bolsheviks

The Bolshevik Party (now the Communist Party) had increased its membership, but it was a different Party now. In 1917 60 per cent of members were workers; by 1921 only 40 per cent were. The rest were government officials, for whom Party membership was a good career move. Hundreds of Party members and their families lived in luxury in the Kremlin, with access to plenty of food and fuel.

The Party was losing what had been their main sources of support: workers and soldiers.

We have now come full circle to the mutiny of Kronstadt sailors at the beginning of this chapter on page 116. Lenin called the mutiny *'the flash of lightning which lit up reality'*. He could see that changes had to be made.

■ Concluding your Enquiry

1 Here again are the seven features of Communist dictatorship listed at the beginning of this chapter.

- The only party permitted was the Communist Party. All other parties were banned.
- The Communist Party was centralised, controlled from the top, with no debate. It controlled all local and central government.
- Censorship was strict. Only Communist newspapers were published.
- The *Cheka* arrested, tortured and executed anyone suspected of opposition.
- Strict discipline was imposed in the Red Army.
- Factory workers had to do what they were ordered.
- Armed squads of *Cheka* went into the villages to seize the grain produced by the peasants.

Look back over your notes on the growth of Communist dictatorship.

a) Which were already under way before the Civil War started?

b) Which were developed during the Civil War under War Communism?

Are there any features which began before the Civil War, but developed more fully during it?

2 This is the hypothesis you have been considering:

The Civil War forced the Communists to become dictators in order to ensure their own, and the Revolution's, survival.

Over the course of this chapter you have found evidence of the growth of Communist dictatorship between 1917 and 1921 under three headings: The growth of Bolshevik dictatorship, the Civil War and War Communism.

You should have found some evidence both for (the need to win a desperate Civil War) and against (the Bolsheviks' long-standing view of the role of their party) our hypothesis. But which is more important?

Here are some things to think about as you reach your judgement on this:

- Chronology. When did the features of dictatorship begin? Was this before the crisis really got under way?
- Are there links between the different aspects of dictatorship?
- How did the dictatorship change over time? In what ways was Russia under more dictatorial rule in 1921 than it was in early 1918?

What do I think?

This question has to be put in the context of all you have read in earlier chapters of this book. The Bolsheviks believed in a theory, Marxism, which accepted struggle against their enemies as normal. They had faced tsarist oppression for decades and seen fellow revolutionaries executed (including Lenin's brother). A Bolshevik leader in the city of Baku wrote: *'Civil war is the same as class war ... we are supporters of civil war, not because we thirst for blood, but because without struggle the oppressors will not give up their privileges to the people.'*

Lenin and the Bolsheviks were also scornful of democracy and democratic values too. You will have seen in this chapter that several of the features of Communist dictatorship began and were well-established before the Civil War proper began. But the brutal Civil War certainly brought a callousness towards human life which was not so evident before. The tragedy was that it became embedded in Soviet Communism for many years to come.

Why did the Reds win the Civil War against the Whites?

Although, as we have seen, the Civil War was a complex set of conflicts, the Whites did present the main military threat to the Bolsheviks. This table, however, sets out the clear advantages the Reds had over the Whites.

	WHITES	REDS
GEOGRAPHY	The map on page 126 shows clearly that White armies were separated from each other by huge distances and could not co-ordinate their military actions. The areas the Whites held had little industry and poor transport links. White areas were also thinly populated, so they could not recruit easily.	The Reds held the heartlands of Russia. This gave them control of: • the two greatest cities, Moscow and Petrograd • most of the railway system • most of Russian industry, especially the armaments industry • more heavily-populated areas • the weapons and supplies of the Tsar's army.
SUPPORT	The Whites failed to provide an attractive vision of a future which would win popular support. • Most of the Whites were tsarists and wanted to put the clock back to before the revolution. • In areas under their control they took land back from the peasants and handed it to the former landlords. • Many were deeply anti-Semitic: up to 50,000 Jews were massacred by White armies. • Whites wanted to restore the boundaries of the Russian Empire to what they had been in 1917. They therefore opposed nationalists (for example in the Ukraine), who then fought against them.	• The peasants did not want to be dragged away to fight, and hated both sides. However, the Reds assured them that the land they had taken over would stay theirs, so they were more inclined to support them. • Factory workers and soldiers had reservations about the Reds, e.g. over War Communism (see below). However, the Reds seemed the best guarantee of the gains made by the Revolution. • Reds were much more pragmatic about the nationalists' desire for independence.
MILITARY STRENGTH	White armies were quite small: Yudenich had perhaps 14,000 men, Denikin never more than 100,000. There were always too many officers and not enough men.	By the end of 1919 the Red Army numbered 1,500,000; by the end of 1920 Trotsky had 3,500,000 soldiers under his command. His problem was shortage of officers (see below).
LEADERSHIP	The ex-tsarist White generals treated their armies with the same contempt which had turned so many soldiers into revolutionaries during the First World War. Many soldiers in the White armies deserted.	Trotsky was a brilliant inspirational leader who turned the Red Army into a formidable force.
ORGANISATION	The lack of unity among the anti-Bolsheviks meant that they failed to work together.	War Communism: a number of drastic measures, using force against workers and peasants taken by Lenin and the Bolsheviks.
PROPAGANDA	White leaders underestimated the importance of winning popular support through propaganda.	The Communists gave considerable attention to propaganda, through posters, films, speakers. There was even a propaganda train to carry the Communist message to the villages.
FOREIGN HELP	Foreign governments provided money and weapons, but not enough to ensure victory.	Foreign support for the Whites allowed the Reds to portray themselves as more patriotic.

Trotsky

The right-hand column of the table would seem to suggest that the balance of advantage lay with the Reds. But their advantages had to be translated into action on the battlefields, and the person who did that was Trotsky.

Early in 1918 the Red Army was formed. Recruits were promised food and pay, and in the conditions in Russia at the time, that was enough to persuade 100,000 to join. They were a rabble. They had few weapons, no uniforms, no training, no ranks and were run by elected committees. They tended to desert when things got rough, or the harvest needed bringing in. This was the raw material which Trotsky turned into the victorious Red Army.

He realised that he needed officers and that he had to turn to the old Imperial army to find them. To ensure their loyalty he attached to each commander a political commissar, a committed Bolshevik, and also took their families hostage. He reintroduced ranks, saluting, and strict discipline, including the death penalty. He told them: *'I issue this warning. If any detachment retreats without orders, the first to be shot will be the commissar, the second will be the commander'*. He was prepared to promote good commanders whatever their age or social origin and created an élite of special forces, in black leather uniforms.

He did not take military decisions, but showed considerable personal bravery. In his famous special train he would rush to critical military situations, inspiring soldiers who were on the point of retreat, raising morale and turning probable defeat into victory. He explained:

> Even after defeats and retreats the panicky, flabby mob would be transformed in two or three weeks into an efficient fighting force. What was needed for this? At once both much and a little. It needed good commanders, a few dozen experienced fighters, a dozen or so communists ready to make any sacrifice, boots, a bath-house, an energetic propaganda campaign, food, underwear, tobacco and matches. The train took care of all this. We always had in reserve a few zealous communists to fill the gaps, a hundred or so good fighting men, leather jackets, medicines, machine-guns, binoculars, maps, watches and all sorts of gifts.

◁ Trotsky rallying Red Army soldiers during the Civil War.

8 Conclusion

What happened next? 1921–24

At the end of Chapter 7 we looked at the plight of the Russian people in 1921, in the cities, in the countryside and in the Party. Following the 'flash of lightning' of the Kronstadt Mutiny, the Communist leadership announced the New Economic Policy (NEP) in March 1921.

- Grain requisitioning by force was stopped and replaced by a tax, which could be paid in grain. It was fixed at a lower level than the grain requisitions. Peasants were allowed to sell their surplus.
- The next step was to allow small-scale private businesses to reopen. This was to encourage the flow of manufactured goods on to the market for peasants to buy and so encourage them to sell food for cash.
- An open market meant that private trade, shops and markets were permitted again.
- Heavy industry (coal, steel, oil) as well as banking, transport and foreign trade remained in government hands.

This was a return to capitalism and many Communists hated it. They were quite clear that it was not what they wanted, but had been forced into. Lenin compared NEP to making the Treaty of Brest Litovsk: an unfortunate necessity in order to stay in power.

By restoring the profit motive to trade and business in Russia, NEP oiled the wheels of trade efficiently and rapidly. Even by 1922, markets had reopened in the cities and food was available, soon followed by other goods as well. '*Nepmen*', small traders, made contact with peasants and bought up their surplus food produce. They sold this in the cities, then bought up manufactured items (boots, clothes, tools) and sold them to the peasants. Deals were made; bribes were offered and taken; successful entrepreneurs flashed their new-found wealth. An American writer, Walter Duranty, described the changing scene on his street:

> One morning I saw a man sitting on the sidewalk selling flour, sugar and rice on a little table … At the end of the week his table had doubled in size and he was selling fresh eggs and vegetables. [Soon] he had rented a tiny shop across the street, handling milk, vegetables, chickens and the freshest eggs and apples in Moscow … By the following May he had four salesmen in a fair-sized store, to which peasants brought produce each morning … In July he added hardware and in October he sold out … to buy a farm …

By 1926 agricultural production, industrial production, coal and textile production had recovered to 1913 levels, and electricity production was running ahead of the pre-war figure. Lenin was keen to provide electric power all over Russia, to every village, as a means of modernisation (see poster).

Communist control

Do not make the mistake of thinking that this freeing up of economic life was accompanied by a freeing up of political life: far from it.

- All other parties were still banned. Menshevik and SR leaders were put on trial in 1922 and several executed.
- The Party was controlled by the Politburo, a small inner ruling group. In 1921 the Party agreed a 'ban on factions'. This put an end to internal Party debate. Party officials at lower levels carried out their own versions of central policies.
- The Communist Party wanted to ensure that only loyal, reliable Party members filled all the important jobs in the government and the Party. A list of 5500 positions, called *nomenklatura*, was drawn up and only people on the approved list could take these positions.
- The Communist Party took over the soviets all over Russia. Soviet officials were no longer elected but appointed by the Party. From 1926, non-Communists were not allowed to stand for election.
- Trade unions were also under Communist Party control, their officials now appointed by the Party.
- The *Cheka* was re-named the GPU (Main Political Administration) in 1922, and increased in size and influence.
- Censorship increased. All books, plays, poems had to be submitted to the censor before they could be published. Film-makers and composers had to conform to Party rules.
- There was a religious revival under NEP, which the Communists crushed. Priests were arrested, churches sacked and many demolished. Anti-religious lessons were part of the school curriculum.
- The USSR was set up in 1922, with a new constitution including Russia and neighbouring communist republics.

△ **This striking poster quotes Lenin's famous slogan:** *'Communism equals Soviet power plus electrification.'*

What happened next? 1924 onwards

The Death of Lenin

Lenin never fully recovered from Fanya Kaplan's assassination attempt in 1918. A bullet was lodged in his brain which doctors could not remove. He suffered a stroke in 1922, and others followed. From March 1923 he was unable to speak much, or walk unaided. He was looked after by his wife until his death on 24 January 1924. His body was embalmed and can still be seen in his tomb in front of the Kremlin in Red Square, Moscow.

It is hard to separate the cult of Lenin, the worship of the great hero-leader, from the reality of the man. Whatever the myths perpetuated later, he was never an all-powerful leader in the same way that Hitler and Stalin were; he was no 'Communist Tsar'. Indeed, until well into 1918 he was able to walk around the streets unrecognised. Within the Party his powerful personality and intellect made him the undisputed leader, but that didn't mean there was no debate or disagreement. Throughout the twists and turns of events of 1917 they wrangled over how the Bolsheviks should act. It was only when the very continuation of their government was threatened in the Civil War that they closed ranks. He was 53 when he became incapable. There is endless speculation over what might have happened if he had lived longer, but by then power was slipping into other hands.

You would have thought that Lenin's obvious successor was Trotsky. But the other leading Bolsheviks resented him and he made little effort to win support. Over the next four years he was outmanoeuvred by Stalin, forced out of the Communist Party, then out of the USSR.

The Russian Revolution in history

I hope that this book has helped you make your own way through the cataclysmic events of the Russian Revolution, examining your own ideas about history and about politics on your journey. Do you see what I meant when I wrote, *'Tell me what you think of the Russian Revolution and I'll tell you who you are'* on page 17?

These were indeed cataclysmic events, affecting world politics for most of the rest of the twentieth century. We have seen that it was the tensions caused by modernisation in an antiquated political system that were at the root of the Russian Revolution. But these same tensions were to be played out in different ways in many parts of the world in the twentieth century. Russia was not the only country where ordinary people found themselves oppressed and had no way of righting their situation peacefully. For many people, on every continent, the Russian Revolution was a model to be studied and learned from. The history of the twentieth century was punctuated by Communist rebellions and revolutions, many successful, some not. Here are just a few of the most well-known:

1918: Communist revolutions in Germany (Berlin, Bavaria and Ruhr), Hungary and Finland; all failed.

1927: Communist rising in Shanghai fails.

1946: Communist governments take over Yugoslavia, Albania.

1948: Communists start civil war in Malaya – defeated.

1949: Communist government set up in China.
Communists start civil war in Greece – defeated.

1954: Communist government set up in North Vietnam.

1959: Cuban Revolution (becomes Communist government 1961).

1970: Communist government elected in Chile (overthrown 1973).

1975: Communist government takes over rest of Vietnam.

1978: Communist government set up in Afghanistan.

1979: Communist government elected in Nicaragua.

Add to these the puppet Communist governments which were set up in the wake of the victorious Red Army after the Second World War:

1946: Lithuania, Latvia, Estonia, Poland, Bulgaria, East Germany, North Korea.

1947: Romania, Hungary.

1948: Czechoslovakia.

While some people wanted to copy the Russian Revolution, for others it was something to be dreaded and fought against. The fate of the rulers of Russia and the financial ruin of those who had owned property and businesses there, was a terrible lesson for the world's better off. Communism was also atheist, so religions across the world fought hard against it. The success of the Fascists in Spain and Italy and, most of all, the rise of Hitler and the Nazis in Germany, was largely because they offered a bulwark against Communism. I don't find 'What ifs' in history very interesting, but you could argue that without the Russian Revolution there would have been no Hitler.

Gorbachev and the end of Communism

In the end, Communism in Russia failed. By the 1960s, as western capitalism was booming, the Soviet economy was stagnant. It just did not seem to be able to deliver the kind of lifestyle – especially personal freedom and quality consumer goods – which everybody, including the Russian people, wanted. After years of drift, Mikhail Gorbachev became General Secretary of the Communist Party in 1985. He wanted to modernise the USSR, bringing in greater personal and economic freedom. But his reforms opened the floodgates to much greater changes than he had intended. In 1991 the Communist Party was banned, the 'satellite' states declared independence and the USSR fell apart. The great Bolshevik experiment had ended.

Historians and the Russian Revolution

This book has followed developments in historical research and writing from 1917 onwards quite closely. What are historians' current concerns? The last fifteen years have seen a number of studies of the Revolution in provincial cities, towns and villages. Historians are just beginning to pull these together to see if our 'big picture' needs modifying.

What seems to be emerging is that the Revolution in the provinces was rather different away from the urban, male, ethnically Russian élites of Moscow and Petrograd. As Sarah Badcock put it, in 2007:

> Explanations for the failure of democratic politics in Russia can now be found not only in the ineptitudes of Nicholas II, the failings of Kerensky, or the machinations of Lenin and his cohort. Instead, ordinary people, outside the capitals and in the countryside, defined and determined revolutionary events.

For one thing, party labels were much less important, and less reliable indicators of beliefs, than we have supposed. Voters in the Constituent Assembly elections in November 1917 took their democratic responsibilities very seriously: there was a 90 per cent turnout in some areas. But candidates tended to be chosen for their character and probity, rather than their party allegiance. Traditional views on gender and ethnicity worked against the selection of ethnic minority or women candidates: in Kazan, for example, only 3 of the 93 candidates were women.

Interestingly, 'Dual Power' might have been an issue in Petrograd, but in many of the provinces Provisional Government officials and soviets worked well together, recognising the need for order and stability. There was also a considerable gap between the rhetoric of Party propaganda and how it was perceived and understood locally. And overall, the problems of food supply outweighed other considerations.

Is this the only book you should read?

Never rely on just one book even if it claims it's the only book you need. Reading other books helps you develop the deeper knowledge and understanding which is vital for success at A level.

This book was written for A level students and was up to date with the latest research by historians when it was published in 2012. I was chosen to write it because I am a writer and I've been a schoolteacher who taught the Russian Revolution at A level for a number of years. But I'm not a historian whose main job is to research this topic, so to keep me up to date with current research scholarship I worked with Matthias Neumann, Senior Lecturer in History at the University of East Anglia, and a working research historian.

Which other books should you read? Ideally not another book written just for A level but a book that takes you deeper. Here are the books I found most useful while writing this book. I have added a few comments to each which I hope will help you decide where you go next.

Edward Acton, *Rethinking the Russian Revolution* (1990). This is very good at explaining the different interpretations of the Russian Revolution, how they arose and why they are different.

Rex A. Wade (editor), *Revolutionary Russia: New Approaches* (2004). This book is an opportunity to see a range of recent research as it includes essays by several key historians. Look especially at Wade's Introduction and the essays by Steve Smith, Diane Koenker & William Rosenberg, and Orlando Figes.

Orlando Figes: *A People's Tragedy* (1996). This is big book – over 900 pages – so unless you are beginning a medium term prison sentence, don't try reading it from cover to cover! Instead, use the Index to read more about the key events and people which interest you. Figes' knowledge, his stories, and his ability to link events among the élite in Petrograd with the peasants in the village of Andreevskoe make this a hugely enjoyable book.

Websites

Seventeen Moments in Soviet History: www.soviethistory.org/

Clicking on one of the 'Moments' produces an excellent variety of short essays, documents, videos, music and so on.

The Prokudin-Gorskii photographic record: www.loc.gov/exhibits/empire/
If you want to know what tsarist Russia looked like, its people, towns and landscapes, scan through these extraordinary photographs. As you will realise, I drew on it for the descriptions of a railway journey across Russia in Chapter 1.

The publication dates are always placed alongside a book title. You should always check these. Why? Think of the changes in history-writing about the Russian Revolution described in this book. Without the date of publication you can't know where a book fits into the development of writing about this topic.

Insight

Index

Acknowledgements

Photo credits

Cover © Andris T – Fotolia; **p.4** © Library of Congress, Prints & Photographs Division, Prokudin-Gorskii Collection (LC-DIG-prokc-20023); **p.5** © Library of Congress, Prints & Photographs Division, Prokudin-Gorskii Collection (LC-DIG-ppmsc-04422); **p.6** © The Granger Collection/TopFoto; **p.7** © Village meeting (sepia photo), Russian Photographer, (20th century)/Private Collection/The Stapleton Collection/The Bridgeman Art Library; **p.8** © RIA Novosti/TopFoto; **p.10** © Library of Congress, Prints & Photographs Division, Prokudin-Gorskii Collection (LC-DIG-prokc-21166); **p.12** © Library of Congress, Prints & Photographs Division, Prokudin-Gorskii Collection (LC-DIG-prokc-20948); **p.13** © akg-images/RIA Nowosti; **p.15** © 2008 Mary Evans Picture Library; **p.16** © The Granger Collection, NYC/TopFoto; **p.17** © RIA Novosti/TopFoto; **p.18** © Illustrated London News; **p.19** *l* © RIA Novosti/TopFoto, *r* © Library of Congress Prints and Photographs Division, Soyuzfoto; **p.20** © Illustrated London News; **p.22** © Christopher Culpin; **p.25** © Illustrated London News; **p.26** © Bettmann/Corbis; **p.27** © Illustrated London News; **p.28** © Hulton Archive/Getty Images; **p.29** © RIA Novosti/TopFoto; **p.30** © RIA Novosti/TopFoto; **p.32** *l* & *r* © RIA Novosti/TopFoto; **p.34** © The Granger Collection, NYC/TopFoto; **p.37** © 2006 RIA Novosti/TopFoto; **p.38** © akg-images; **p.39** © Library of Congress, Prints & Photographs Division, Prokudin-Gorskii Collection (LC-DIG-prokc-21479); **p.40** © Corbis; **p.42** © Library of Congress, Prints & Photographs Division, Prokudin-Gorskii Collection (LC-DIG-prokc-20542); **p.48** © Illustrated London News; **p.49** © Christopher Culpin; **p.50** © RIA Novosti/TopFoto; **p.53** © 2008 Mary Evans Picture Library © DACS 2012; **p.54** © Hulton Archive/Getty Images; **p.57** © electrons_fishgils http://www.flickr.com/photos/42186300@N07/4004822205/sizes/l/in/photostream/ Creative Commons http://creativecommons.org/licenses/by/2.0/; **p.58** © Library of Congress, Prints & Photographs Division, Prokudin-Gorskii Collection (LC-DIG-prokc-20720); **p.62** © RIA Novosti / TopFoto; **p.66** © Photas/Tass/Press Association Images; **p.68** © Bettmann/Corbis; **p.70** © Hulton-Deutsch Collection/Corbis; **p.71** © The Print Collector/Alamy; **p.72** © Illustrated London News; **p.73** © David King Collection; **p.77** © Christopher Culpin; **p.78** © Fine Art Images/Heritage Images; **p.84** © World History Archive/TopFoto; **p.86** © Alena Kovalenko – Fotolia; **p.88** © MosFilms/Ronald Grant Archive; **p.98** © Popperfoto/Getty Images; **p.114** © Illustrated London News; **p.120** © Library of Congress Prints and Photographs Division, Soyuzfoto; **p.130** © Hulton-Deutsch Collection/Corbis; **p.131** © Christopher Culpin; **p.133** © Popperfoto/Getty Images; **p.135** © Fine Art Images/SuperStock.

Text credits

p.23, **106** Steve A. Smith, *The Worker's Revolution in Russia*, 1917 (Cambridge University Press, 1987; Cambridge Books Online, 2007); **p.26, 27, 54–55, 112** Orlando Figes, *A People's Tragedy: The Russian Revolution 1891–1924* (Pimlico, 1996), reproduced by permission of The Random House Group; **p.27** Sarah Badcock, *Politics and the People in Russia: A Provincial History* (Cambridge University Press, 2007); **p.82** W. H. Chamberlain, *The Russian Revolution* (1935); **p.85** John Reed, *Ten Days That Shook the World*; **p.89** Richard Pipes, *The Russian Revolution 1899–1919* (Fontana Press, 1992); **p.105 & 106** figures for graphs from Diane Koenker and William Rosenburg, in *Revolution in Russia*, ed. Frankel, Frankel and Krei-Paz (Cambridge, 1992); **p.108** John Channon, 'The Peasantry in the Revolutions of 1917' in *Revolution in Russia: re-assessment of 1917*, ed. E. R. Frankel et al; **p.114 & 133** Leon Trotsky, *History of the Russian Revolution*; **p.134** Walter Duranty, *Duranty reports Russia*; **p.138** Sarah Badcock, 'The Russian Revolution: Broadening Understandings of 1917' in *The History Compass* (2007).

Every effort has been made to trace all copyright holders, but if any have been inadvertently overlooked, the Publishers will be pleased to make the necessary arrangements at the first opportunity.